SIMPLE & DELICIOUS
CHINESE
COOKING

SIMPLE & DELICIOUS
CHINESE COOKING

Deh-ta Hsiung

CONTENTS

ANOTHER BEST-SELLING VOLUME FROM HPBooks®

Publisher: Rick Bailey; Editorial Director: Retha M. Davis
Editor: Jeanette P. Egan; Art Director: Don Burton
Book Assembly: Kathleen Koopman
Book Manufacture: Anthony B. Narducci
Typography: Cindy Coatsworth, Michelle Claridge
Recipe testing by International Cookbook Services: Barbara Bloch,
President; Rita Barrett, Director of Testing

Notice: The information contained in this book is true and complete to the best of
our knowledge. All recommendations are made without any guarantees on the
part of the author or HPBooks. The author and publisher disclaim all liability in
connection with the use of this information.

Published by HPBooks, Inc.
P.O. Box 5367, Tucson, AZ 85703   602/888-2150
ISBN 0-89586-338-3
Library of Congress Catalog Card Number 84-81921
©1985 HPBooks, Inc.   Printed in the U.S.A.
1st Printing

Originally published as Chinese Cookery
©1983 Hennerwood Publications Limited

Cover Photo: Fish Slices with Wine Sauce, page 49;
Three Sea Flavors and Phoenix-Tail Shrimp, page 48.

Introduction

Trade and cultural exchanges between China and the outside world took place as early as the time of the Roman Empire. However, Chinese culinary art was comparatively unknown in the West until recent times.

Many people have always wanted to try Chinese cooking. However, they have been discouraged by the thought of exotic ingredients and complicated techniques. These are unfounded fears. Basic Chinese cooking is really quite simple. In this book there are recipes representing a wide range of China's various regional styles. Also included are a number of dishes that could be termed specialties. They are not elaborate or time-consuming.

An authentic Chinese meal is a multi-course affair. For this reason, menu planning is different from planning a Western menu. In China, several dishes may be served at the same time. Recipes in this book are arranged to simplify the process of planning menus. Dishes may be used for an all-Chinese meal or as part of a Western-style meal.

Since not all Chinese ingredients are available in this country, adequate substitutes are suggested when possible. A Chinese cook, anywhere in the world, can always produce a Chinese meal, using only local ingredients. The authentic Chinese flavor of the food depends more on how it is prepared and cooked, not what ingredients are used.

REGIONAL COOKING STYLES

The fundamentals of Chinese cooking remain the same throughout China. All food is prepared and cooked in accordance with the same principles. These principles include careful preparation of ingredients before cooking, heat control and harmonious blending of different flavors. This is true from Peking cuisine in the north to Cantonese cooking in the south. What distinguishes one region from the other is the staple food and special seasoning. For example, in the north, people eat more wheat products, such as noodles, dumplings and pancakes. In the south, more rice and rice products are the foundation of the diet.

Traditionally, the various styles of cooking are classified into four major groups according to locality.

The eastern region is represented by China's largest city, Shanghai, with a population of well over 12 million. The cuisine of Shanghai is strongly influenced by the regional styles from the Yangtse River delta, particularly by the sophisticated school known as Huaiyang. The characteristics of this region can be best summarized as exquisite in appearance, rich in flavor and sweet in taste.

The southern region is represented by China's most diverse school of cuisine, originating from Canton in the Pearl River delta. Because Canton was the first Chinese port opened for trade, foreign influences are particularly strong in its cooking. Together with the neighboring province of Fujian, Canton is the origin of many Chinese emigrants. Therefore, this is also the best-known style of Chinese cooking abroad.

The western region is characterized by the richly flavored and piquant food of Szechuan. Before the discovery of chili pepper in the New World, the less pungent but numbing Szechuan peppercorn was the dominant spicy flavor. Now chili peppers and peppercorns are both used extensively. The neighboring province of Hunan is also renowned for hot, peppery cooking.

The northern region is centered around Peking, China's capital for many centuries. Because it is the political and cultural center of China, Peking has accumulated the best cooking styles from all the other regions. It has become China's culinary center in addition to creating a cuisine of its own. Fermented sauces are important in this region. Lamb is more popular here than in other regions.

You will find recipes from each of these regions in this book. A few recipes have been slightly adapted for practical reasons, but the majority are unaltered to preserve their authenticity.

CHARACTERISTICS OF CHINESE COOKING

The most distinctive feature in Chinese cooking is harmonious balance of colors, aromas, flavors and form in a single dish.

Color (se)—Each ingredient has its own color. Many foods change color when cooked. This is important to remember when selecting ingredients for the blending of colors.

Aroma (xiang)—Each ingredient has its own aroma or fragrance—some sharp, some subtle. Most meats and fish have a rather distinct smell. They need a seasoning agent to enhance their aroma when cooked. Chinese rice wine is used for this purpose. Dry sherry is a good substitute for rice wine. Other widely used seasonings are green onions, gingerroot and garlic.

Flavor (wei)—Flavor is closely related to aroma and color. The principle of blending complementary flavors is fundamental. The matching of flavors follows a set pattern and is controlled, not casual. Different ingredients must not be mixed indiscriminately.

Form (xing)—The shape of cut ingredients is important in achieving the proper effect. All ingredients are cut into slices, shreds, cubes and so on. This is not just for the sake of appearance, which is an important element of Chinese culinary art, but because ingredients of the same size and shape require about the same amount of cooking time.

This complexity of interrelated elements of color, aroma, flavor and form in Chinese cooking is reinforced by yet another feature: *texture*. A dish may have one or several textures, such as tenderness, crispness, crunchiness, smoothness and softness. The textures to be avoided are: sogginess, stringiness and hardness. The selection of different textures in one dish is an integral part of blending flavors and colors.

PREPARATION & COOKING TECHNIQUES
Slicing—This is probably the most common form of cutting in Chinese cooking. To slice, ingredients are cut into 1/8-inch slices. The slices are then cut into 1-1/2-inch by 1-inch pieces. It is easier to slice uncooked meats if they are first partially frozen.

Shredding—Shredding is similar to the julienne technique. To shred, first cut ingredients into thin slices. Stack slices; cut into thin strips about size of wooden matchsticks (1/8 inch by 1/8 inch).

Dicing—To dice, first cut ingredients into coarse strips about 1/4 inch by 1/4 inch; then dice into 1/4-inch cubes.

Diagonal cutting—This method is used for cutting vegetables, such as carrots, celery, zucchini or asparagus. Make a vertical diagonal cut; roll vegetable half a turn before making next cut.

Mincing or finely chopping—Chop ingredients into small bits. Although a food processor or blender can be used, flavor and texture will not be quite the same.

Map of the four main culinary regions of China

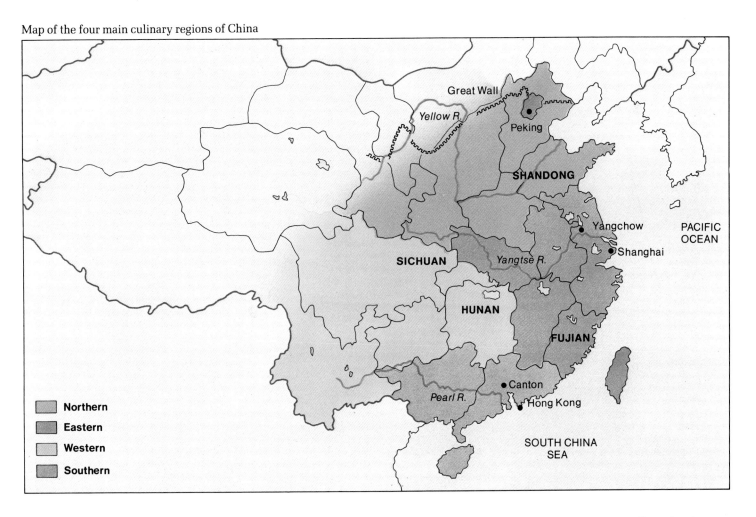

Northern

Eastern

Western

Southern

Flower-cutting—First diagonally score surface of each piece in a crisscross pattern. Then cut into small pieces. When cooked, each piece will open up and resemble ears of corn or flowers, hence the name *flower*. Kidneys, squid and tripe are usually cut in this manner.

Chopping—To cut a whole cooked chicken or duck across the bones, follow these directions:

1. Remove wings, legs and thighs.
2. Separate breast from back.
3. Chop back into about 8 pieces; place on bottom of a serving dish. Chop each wing into 2 or 3 pieces; place on each side of back pieces.
4. Chop each leg and thigh into 3 or 4 pieces; place on edge of serving dish.
5. Split breast lengthwise; cut each half into 3 or 4 pieces. Arrange on top of back pieces.

After cutting, the next step in Chinese food preparation is seasoning or coating. The basic method for coating fish or chicken is to combine fish or chicken with salt, egg white and cornstarch. This technique, known as *velveting*, preserves the natural delicate texture during cooking in hot oil. Meat is combined with salt, sugar, soy sauce, rice wine and cornstarch.

To achieve the desired texture or textures in any dish, use the correct cooking method. There are four basic cooking techniques: water-cooking, oil-cooking, steam-cooking and fire-cooking.

1/Remove wings; then remove legs and thighs.

2/Separate breast from backbone.

3/Cut each wing into 2 to 3 pieces.

4/Split breast down the middle.

Top to bottom: above bowl, cellophane noodles; bamboo shoots; light soy sauce; bean sprouts; soaked and dry wood ears; hot bean paste; egg noodles

WATER-COOKING

Chuan—Rapid boiling over a high heat. Thinly sliced or shredded ingredients are dropped into boiling stock or water to be cooked for only 1 to 2 minutes. Cook most soup dishes this way.

Zhu—Boiling over medium heat under cover. Use this method for dishes requiring long cooking, such as *Salted Peking Duck*, page 20, and casserole dishes.

Dun—Simmering over a low heat under cover. See *Crystal-Boiled Pork*, page 22, or *Lion's Head*, page 62.

Qiang—Blanching in boiling water, then dressing with sauce. See *Peking Poached Shrimp*, page 14.

OIL-COOKING

Chao—Stir-frying over high heat. Thinly sliced or shredded ingredients are stir-fried in a few tablespoons of hot oil for a short time.

Bao—Rapid-frying over extreme heat. Bao literally means to explode. See *Rapid-Fried Shrimp in Shells*, page 14, or *Rapid-Fried Lamb Slices*, page 42.

Zha—Deep-frying over a medium heat.

Jian—Shallow-frying over medium heat. This method uses more oil than stir-frying but less than deep-frying.

Shao—Stewing over a low heat; see *Spiced Beef*, page 22.

Lu—Soy-braising; see *Braised Tripe*, page 20.

Hui—Another form of braising. Hui literally means "assembly." Normally a number of ingredients, some cooked, some semi-cooked, are blended together for the final stage of cooking in sauce. See *Chicken Wings Assembly*, page 57.

STEAM-COOKING

Zheng—Steaming. In Chinese cooking, there are two methods of steaming. In the first, a plate or bowl containing ingredients is placed on the bottom rack of a steamer. Then the steamer is placed inside a wok containing boiling water. Food is cooked by steam passing through the steamer. The second method is to place the plate or bowl containing the ingredients on a wire or bamboo rack that fits inside a wok containing boiling water. The wok is covered; again food is cooked by steam rising inside the wok. Non-Chinese steamers can be used.

FIRE-COOKING

Kao—Roasting in an oven.

Cha Shao—Barbecuing on an open fire.

SPECIAL INGREDIENTS & SEASONINGS

To produce a Chinese meal, special ingredients are not always needed. However, there are certain items that are commonly available that will add an exotic touch to everyday cooking.

Bamboo shoots—Ivory-colored shoots of bamboo plants. They are available canned. After opening, cover with water, seal and refrigerate up to a week.

Bean curd—Also known as dofu or tofu. This custard-like preparation of pureed and pressed soybeans is exceptionally high in protein. In China, it is known as the "poor man's meat." It is sold in cakes about 3 inches square and 1 to 3 inches thick. It is available in Oriental markets and supermarkets. Cover it with water and store in the refrigerator. Use within a few days. Change water daily.

Bean sprouts—Sprouts from mung beans. Fresh bean sprouts are widely available in most supermarkets. Refrigerate two to three days. Do not use canned bean sprouts. They do not have the crunchy texture that is characteristic of this popular vegetable.

Cellophane or transparent noodles—Dried noodles made from mung beans. They are sold in dried bundles weighing from 2 ounces to 1 pound. Soak in warm water 5 minutes before using.

Hot bean paste—Fermented bean paste mixed with salt, flour and hot chilies. It is sold in jars. Chili sauce mixed with crushed yellow-bean sauce is a substitute. The amount of chili sauce used depends entirely on personal taste.

Chili sauce—Hot red sauce made from chilies, vinegar, sugar and salt. Use sparingly in cooking or as a dipping sauce. Substitute hot-pepper sauce, if desired.

Dried Chinese mushrooms—Widely used in many dishes for flavor and aroma. Soak in warm water 20 to 30 minutes, or in cold water several hours or until softened. When mushrooms are softened, rinse and squeeze dry. Discard hard stems before using. Dried European mushrooms, though of slightly different flavor and fragrance, can be substituted.

Cooking oil—In China, usually peanut oil. Use any good vegetable oil.

Dried shrimp—Salted and sun-dried shrimp. They are available in various sizes. Soak in warm water about 30 minutes or until softened. Drain and rinse before using. Store indefinitely in a dry, air-tight container.

Five-spice powder—A mixture of star anise, fennel seeds, cloves, cinnamon and Szechuan pepper. It is very piquant; use sparingly. Keep tightly covered.

Gingerroot—Sold fresh in most supermarkets. Refrigerated, it will keep for weeks. Do not substitute powdered ginger.

Hoisin sauce—Also known as *barbecue sauce*. This piquant sauce is made from soy sauce, sugar, flour, vinegar, salt, garlic, chili and sesame oil. Refrigerated, it will keep several months.

Oyster sauce—Thickish brown sauce made from oysters and soy sauce. This bottled sauce will keep several months if refrigerated.

Red-bean paste—Reddish-brown paste made from pureed red beans and sugar. It is sold in cans. Once opened, transfer to a covered container. It will keep in the refrigerator several months. Substitute sweetened chestnut puree.

Rice wine—Also known as *Shaohsing wine*. It is made from glutinous rice. Substitute dry sherry.

Salted black beans—Very salty indeed! Also known as *fermented black beans*. They are sold in plastic bags, jars or cans. Crush with water or rice wine before using. They will keep indefinitely in a tightly covered jar.

Sesame paste—Sold in jars covered with oil. It resembles clay in color and consistency, but is aromatic, rich and tasty. Stir to incorporate oil before using. Substitute peanut butter creamed with sesame

Sesame oil—Oil from sesame seeds. It is sold in bottles. In China, it is widely used for seasoning rather than cooking. The refined yellow-sesame oil sold in Middle Eastern stores is not as aromatic, has less flavor and is not a very satisfactory substitute.

Szechuan peppercorns—Also known as *hua chiao*. This reddish-brown peppercorn is much stronger and more fragrant than black or white peppercorns. They are sold in plastic bags. Store peppercorns in a tightly sealed container.

Szechuan preserved vegetable—Specialty of Szechuan. It is the root of a special variety of mustard greens that is pickled in salt and chilies. It is sold in cans. Once opened, preserved vegetable should be transferred, unwashed, to a tightly covered container. Refrigerated, it will keep for months.

Soy sauce—Made from fermented soybeans, wheat, yeast, salt and sugar. Sold in bottles or cans, this popular Chinese sauce is used for cooking and at the table. Use light soy sauce for light meats, chicken and fish. Dark soy sauce is usually sweeter and is used for red meats. It will discolor food more than light soy sauce.

Water chestnuts—Available fresh or in cans. Canned water chestnuts are already peeled. They will keep refrigerated several weeks in fresh water in a covered jar.

Wood ears or cloud ears—Dried black fungus. Soak in warm water 20 minutes; then rinse in fresh water before using. They have a crunchy texture and a mild but subtle flavor.

Yellow-bean sauce—Thick sauce made from crushed yellow beans, flour and salt. It is sold in cans or jars. After opening, transfer to a jar with a lid. It will then keep in the refrigerator for months.

WOKS & OTHER EQUIPMENT

The most frequently used cooking method in China is quick or rapid stir-frying. Use a wok for the best results.

The wok has three main advantages. First, because of its shape, a wok heats evenly. This decreases cooking time. Second, after stirring, ingredients always return to the center. The final advantage is that a smaller amount of oil is needed to cook in a wok than a skillet. The traditional iron wok keeps a steady and intense heat. Woks may also be made of heavy steel.

A new wok should be seasoned before use. First, wash it in hot soapy water; then dry by placing it over medium heat. When dry, add 1 to 2 tablespoons vegetable oil. Carefully rotate and tilt the hot wok to distribute the oil. Leave on the heat about 5 minutes. Turn off heat; leave wok to cool. A note of caution: do not leave a hot wok unattended. When it is cool, wipe excess oil from wok with paper towels.

After each use, always wash the wok immediately. To prevent rusting, dry thoroughly over a medium heat before putting wok away. Follow above directions if your wok needs to be seasoned again.

Besides stir-frying, use the wok for deep-frying, shallow-frying, steaming, braising, stewing and boiling. The type with a single handle is best suited to stir-frying; the two-handled type is better for all other purposes, as it rests more steadily on the burner. Flat-bottomed woks are available for use on electric elements. Flat-bottomed woks are less likely to tip; this is an advantage when deep-frying. Electric woks are a comparatively recent innovation. An electric wok is useful as a second wok or for use at the table. It is safer to use than a charcoal-burning fire-pot when cooking Chinese Hot-Pot, page 70. Some electric woks may not reach a high enough temperature for stir-frying.

It is useful to have a bamboo steamer. The advantage of a bamboo steamer over a metal one is that the bamboo lid is not airtight. This allows a small amount of evaporation, which prevents condensation forming inside the lid. Substitute a rack or a metal steamer if a bamboo steamer is not available.

A cleaver is one of the few essential tools in a Chinese kitchen. It may appear to be dangerous and awkward to use. In reality, it is light, steady and not dangerous to use provided you handle it correctly and with care. With practice, it will be easy and simple to use. Use it as a cutting knife and not a chopper. Special heavy cleavers are available for chopping bones.

Chopsticks are awkward to use at first. However, learning to use them can be great fun. Practice using them, following the illustrations below. Soon you will be using chopsticks with ease for eating and cooking.

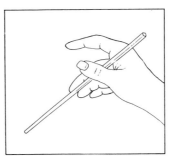

1/Start by placing one chopstick in hollow between thumb and forefinger. Firmly rest lower end of chopstick below first joint of third finger.

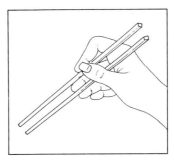

2/Grasp second chopstick between thumb and forefinger, so that its tip is level with first chopstick.

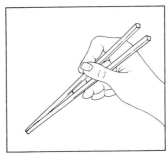

3/To pick up food, keep first chopstick completely still; move only second chopstick.

ART OF MENU PLANNING

The order of courses at a Chinese meal will depend on the cooking method and how ingredients are prepared before cooking. This is different from the typical Western menu sequence.

As previously mentioned, the four most important elements in Chinese cookery are color, aroma, flavor and form. These elements must balance to form a harmonious whole, both in a dish and in a meal of different dishes. Therefore, start the meal with light

Chinese wok with fresh ingredients

and delicate dishes. As the meal progresses, serve rich and spicy dishes.

At a Chinese meal, all diners take food from the serving dishes placed on the table. No one receives an individual serving. The exception is a light snack when a dish of *Chow Mein*, page 72, or a bowl of *Noodles in Soup*, page 72, is served. Then each person is given his or her own portion.

When planning the menu for a dinner party of eight to ten people, start with two cold starters or assorted hors d'oeuvres. Then serve two or three quick stir-fried dishes. Next, serve rice and two or three long-cooked, braised or steamed dishes. A soup can be included, if desired. By varying cooking methods, less time will be spent in the kitchen. For fewer people, reduce the number of dishes.

The following overview of the next five chapters will aid in menu planning. Brief descriptions of each chapter and serving suggestions are included.

Cold Starters & Buffet Dishes

Chinese etiquette is quite different from traditional Western etiquette. A guest is never asked to sit at an empty table. If serving one or more cold dishes as a starter, place them on the table before guests are seated. Prepare the cold dishes in advance to prevent a last-minute rush.

Serve leftovers as assorted hors d'oeuvres, pages 25 and 26. Dishes such as a whole chicken, duck or roast meats are ideal for buffets and parties.

Many of these cold dishes blend well with Western meals. Flexibility and diversity are important aspects of Chinese cooking.

Soups

Water and tea are not often served at meals in China. When tea is served, it is usually at the beginning or end of a meal. Therefore soups, which are served throughout the meal, replace tea and water as thirst-quenchers. On formal occasions or at banquets, soups appear between courses to cleanse the palate.

Chinese soups are mostly clear broths to which thinly sliced or shredded vegetables or meat are added just before serving. The soups in this book make 4 servings.

Stir-Fried Dishes

Stir-fried dishes are the backbone of everyday Chinese cooking. It is an economic way of cooking. The majority of these dishes are made with eight ounces of meat plus vegetables. A single dish will serve at least two people. With two or three other dishes and rice or noodles, each dish will serve six to eight people.

Stir-frying is a quick method of cooking. Thinly sliced or shredded ingredients are tossed and stirred a short time in hot oil over high heat. Meat will cook in 1-1/2 to 2 minutes. Chicken and seafood take even less time. With the right ingredients, a simple but delicious meal of two to three stir-fried dishes for four to six people can be prepared, cooked and served in under one hour! Do all preparation for the different dishes before starting to cook.

Most stir-fried dishes consist of a main ingredient with one or several other ingredients. Select ingredients for harmonious balance of color, aroma, flavor, form and texture.

This chapter includes a few deep-fried and quick-braised dishes for wider variety in menu planning.

Braised & Steamed Dishes

The Chinese do not normally conclude a meal with a sweet course. After cold starters and quick stir-fried dishes, what are called the big dishes are served. These usually require long cooking. Prepare and cook these in advance, if desired.

Some of these dishes are interchangeable with cold starters and buffet dishes. The general rule is that certain dishes are best served cold; therefore, they are grouped together in the first section. Other braised and steamed dishes are best served hot; therefore, they are put in this section. Most of these dishes blend well with Western food. Serve these dishes on their own as a complete meal or in conjunction with non-Chinese food.

Recipes in this section serve four to six people as a main course. As part of a multi-course Chinese meal, they serve eight to ten.

Rice, Noodles & Pancakes

This section includes dishes for the substantial part of a Chinese meal. Most dishes can be served as a light meal or snack. Noodles are always served for birthday celebrations. The Chinese regard the length of noodles as representative of long life.

Serve Spring Rolls, page 77; Dumplings, page 78; or Peking Onion Pancakes, page 76, as a starter or as part of a buffet.

Drinks

Choosing wine to go with a Chinese meal should not present problems. Red or white wine can be served with any Chinese meal. In general, dry or semisweet white wines or light red wines are preferred. Many people prefer to drink beer with Chinese food, particularly the spicy dishes.

Tea should be served at the end of the meal without sugar or milk; it is most refreshing and invigorating.

Brillat-Savarin said that "the discovery of a new dish does more for the happiness of mankind than the discovery of a new star." Perhaps this book will bring you much happiness.

SAMPLE MENU FOR 4 TO 6 PEOPLE

1 or 2 Cold Starters
Peking Poached Shrimp
Kidney Salad
or
Assorted Hors d'Oeuvres (1)

1 or 2 Stir-Fried Dishes
Fish Slices with Wine Sauce
Shredded Chicken Breast with Green Peppers
or
Chicken Cubes with Celery
Cantonese Beef in Oyster Sauce

Braised Dish served with Rice
"Lion's Head" (Pork Meatballs with
Chinese Cabbage)
or
Five-Spice Pork Spareribs
Egg-Drop Soup

Dessert
Fresh Fruit, Ice Cream or Cookies

SAMPLE MENU FOR 8 TO 10 PEOPLE

2 or 3 Cold Starters
Crystal-Boiled Shrimp in Jelly
Salted Peking Duck
Hot & Sour Cabbage
or
Assorted Hors d'Oeuvres (2)

2 or 3 Stir-Fried Dishes
Braised Fish Steak
Diced Chicken in Peking Bean Sauce
Pork Slices with Chinese Vegetables
or
Red & White Shrimp with Green Vegetable
Chicken Cubes with Walnuts Szechuan-Style
Rapid-Fried Lamb Slices

2 or 3 Braised or Steamed Dishes
Lamb & Cucumber Soup
Aromatic & Crispy Szechuan Duck
Cantonese Steamed Sea Bass
or
Steamed Chicken with Mushrooms
Braised Beef
Fish & Bean-Curd Casserole

Dessert
Fruit Salad

Examples of prepared ingredients for Chinese cooking

炝明虾

Peking Poached Shrimp

8 oz. peeled, deveined uncooked shrimp
2 cups water
2 tablespoons rice wine or dry sherry
1 teaspoon salt
2 teaspoons sesame oil

To garnish:
1 tablespoon thinly shredded gingerroot

---

1. If shrimp are frozen, thaw before using. Rinse shrimp. Cut each shrimp in half lengthwise.
2. In a medium saucepan, bring water to a boil. Add shrimp; cook until pink. Drain shrimp; cool in a bowl of cold water a few seconds. Drain well; place shrimp on a small serving dish.
3. In a small bowl, combine wine or sherry, salt and sesame oil; pour mixture evenly over shrimp.
4. Garnish with gingerroot. Serve cold by itself or as part of assorted hors d'oeuvres, pages 25 and 26. Makes about 12 appetizers.

油爆虾

Rapid-Fried Shrimp in Shells

8 oz. unpeeled uncooked shrimp
Vegetable oil for deep-frying
2 tablespoons rice wine or dry sherry
1/2 teaspoon salt
2 tablespoons soy sauce
2 teaspoons sugar
1 teaspoon finely chopped green onion
1 teaspoon finely chopped gingerroot

To garnish:
1 tablespoon finely chopped fresh coriander or parsley

It is easier to eat these shrimp with chopsticks or your fingers than with a fork.

1. Rinse shrimp; remove legs. Do not peel. Pat dry with paper towels.
2. Heat oil in a wok or saucepan over high heat. Deep-fry shrimp until bright pink; quickly remove with a slotted spoon. Carefully pour oil from wok or saucepan; reserve for another use, if desired.
3. Return shrimp to same wok or saucepan; add wine or sherry, salt, soy sauce, sugar, onion and gingerroot. Stir over medium heat until each shrimp is coated with sauce.
4. Neatly arrange shrimp on a serving dish. Garnish with coriander or parsley. Serve hot or cold. Makes about 12 appetizers.

熟炝虾仁

Hot Mixed Shrimp

8 oz. peeled, deveined uncooked shrimp
2 cups water

Sauce:
2 teaspoons cornstarch
1 tablespoon water
1 tablespoon sesame oil
2 tablespoons soy sauce
1 teaspoon sugar

To garnish:
2 teaspoons finely chopped gingerroot

---

1. Rinse shrimp with cold water.
2. In a medium saucepan, bring 2 cups water to a boil. Remove from heat; immediately add shrimp. Cover; steep shrimp 2 to 3 minutes or until pink.
3. Drain shrimp. Place in a serving dish.
4. For sauce, in a small bowl, combine cornstarch and water. Warm sesame oil in a wok or saucepan over medium heat. Stir in soy sauce and sugar until sugar dissolves. Stir in cornstarch mixture. Cook sauce until thickened, stirring constantly. Pour sauce evenly over shrimp.
5. Garnish with gingerroot. Serve cold. Makes about 12 appetizers.

Clockwise from top: Rapid-Fried Shrimp in Shells, light soy sauce, Peking Poached Shrimp, Hot Mixed Shrimp

Shanghai "Smoked" Fish

1-1/2 to 1-3/4 lbs. cod or haddock
3 tablespoons soy sauce
3 tablespoons rice wine or dry sherry
1/2 teaspoon salt
3 or 4 green onions
3 thin gingerroot slices
1 teaspoon five-spice powder
1/4 cup sugar
1/3 cup water
Vegetable oil for deep-frying

This dish is interesting because the fish acquires a smoky flavor without actually being smoked. It is seasoned with soy sauce and wine, then deep-fried in hot oil and finally seasoned in a special sauce.

1. Leave fish in fairly large pieces or it will break up when cooked. In a medium bowl, combine soy sauce, wine or sherry and salt; add fish. Let stand 5 to 10 minutes.
2. Drain any liquid from fish into a small saucepan. Add onions, gingerroot, five-spice powder, sugar and 1/3 cup water. Bring to a boil over medium heat. Simmer about 10 minutes. Strain through a sieve; reserve sauce.
3. Heat oil in a wok or deep-fryer over medium heat. Deep-fry fish pieces in hot oil 4 to 5 minutes or until crisp and golden. Remove fish with a slotted spoon; drain on paper towels.
4. Place drained fish in a medium bowl; pour reserved sauce over fish. Let stand 10 minutes. Serve chilled or at room temperature. Makes 4 servings.

Clockwise from bottom: Crystal-Boiled Shrimp in Jelly, Jellied Chicken, Fish Slices in Hot Sauce

珊 瑚 魚 片

Fish Slices in Hot Sauce

1 (1-lb.) firm white fish
2 tablespoons rice wine or dry sherry
1 teaspoon salt
1 cup vegetable oil
1 medium red bell pepper, shredded
1/2 cup sliced bamboo shoots
2 or 3 green onions, cut into short lengths
1 tablespoon shredded gingerroot
1 teaspoon sugar
1/2 cup Basic Stock, page 28
About 2 teaspoons chili sauce

This is a colorful dish with a piquant flavor. Serve hot or cold.

1. Cut fish into about 12 slices. In a medium bowl, combine fish, wine or sherry and 1/2 teaspoon salt. Let stand 10 minutes.
2. Heat oil in a wok or skillet over medium heat. Add fish slices, one at a time; deep-fry 2 to 3 minutes. Gently remove fish with a slotted spoon; drain on paper towels.
3. Pour off all but 1 tablespoon oil from wok. Return wok to heat; add bell pepper, bamboo shoots, onions and gingerroot. Stir several times; add remaining salt, sugar and stock. Bring to a boil. Add fish slices; reduce heat to low.
4. Cook until liquid is almost evaporated. Add chili sauce to taste; stir until blended. Arrange fish in a serving dish. Makes 4 servings.

凍 鷄

Jellied Chicken

1 (3- to 3-1/2-lb.) roasting chicken
About 7 cups water
2 teaspoons salt
2 tablespoons rice wine or dry sherry
3 green onions
3 thin slices gingerroot

1. In a large saucepan, simmer chicken in water 1 hour or until chicken is tender. Drain chicken, reserving cooking liquid. Remove chicken meat from bones. Discard bones and skin. Place chicken meat in a large heatproof mold.
2. Add salt and wine or sherry. Add enough reserved cooking liquid to cover chicken. Top with onions and gingerroot.
3. Place mold in a steamer or large saucepan. Cover; steam 45 minutes. Remove mold; discard onions and gingerroot.
4. Cool mold slightly; refrigerate 6 to 8 hours or until set.
5. To serve, turn out molded chicken onto a serving dish; remove mold. Makes 4 to 6 servings.

水 晶 明 虾

Crystal-Boiled Shrimp in Jelly

8 oz. peeled, deveined uncooked small shrimp
2 cups chicken stock
2 thin gingerroot slices
1 green onion
1 teaspoon Szechuan or black peppercorns
1 teaspoon salt

Jelly:
1 (1/4-oz.) envelope unflavored gelatin
1/4 cup cold water
Few drops browning sauce, if desired

To garnish:
Cucumber slices

1. In a large saucepan, combine shrimp, stock, gingerroot, onion, peppercorns and salt; bring to a boil. Reduce heat; simmer gently 2 to 3 minutes or until shrimp turn pink.
2. Remove shrimp with a slotted spoon. Arrange in layers in a medium bowl or round mold.
3. For jelly, in a small bowl, combine gelatin and cold water; let stand 3 minutes. Strain stock; discard solid ingredients. Add soaked gelatin to hot strained stock; stir over low heat until gelatin dissolves. Stir in browning sauce, if desired.
4. Pour gelatin mixture over shrimp. Refrigerate 4 to 6 hours or until set.
5. To serve, turn out shrimp mixture onto a serving plate; remove mold. Decorate shrimp jelly with cucumber slices. Makes 1 medium mold.

豉 油 雞 (廣東式)

Cantonese Soya Braised Chicken

1 (3- to 3-1/2-lb.) roasting chicken
2 tablespoons freshly ground Szechuan or black pepper
2 tablespoons finely chopped gingerroot
5 tablespoons dark soy sauce
3 tablespoons rice wine or dry sherry
2 tablespoons sugar
3 tablespoons vegetable oil
1/2 cup water or chicken stock
1 small head lettuce, shredded

This bright brown chicken is seen in restaurant windows in China. Serve hot or cold.

1. Pat chicken dry with paper towels. Rub inside and out with pepper and gingerroot.
2. In a large bowl, combine soy sauce, wine or sherry and sugar. Add chicken; let stand at least 45 minutes, turning several times. Remove chicken from liquid, reserving liquid. Pat chicken dry with paper towels.
3. Heat oil in a wok or large saucepan over medium heat. Add seasoned chicken; sauté until browned. Add reserved liquid and water or stock. Bring to a boil; reduce heat. Cover; simmer 45 minutes, turning chicken several times during cooking without breaking skin.
4. Chop chicken into small pieces. Spread lettuce on a medium platter. Arrange chopped chicken neatly over lettuce. Pour 2 tablespoons cooking liquid over chicken. Refrigerate until ready to serve. Makes 4 to 6 servings.

Left to right: Soya Duck, Szechuan Bang-Bang Chicken

棒 棒 鷄

Szechuan Bang-Bang Chicken

2 boneless chicken breasts
Salt
Water
1 head lettuce, shredded

Sauce:
1 tablespoon sesame-seed paste
1 tablespoon light soy sauce
2 tablespoons vinegar
About 1 teaspoon chili sauce
1 teaspoon sugar
2 tablespoons chicken stock or water

This popular Peking and Szechuan restaurant dish is extremely simple to cook. If sesame-seed paste is not available, an acceptable substitute is peanut butter creamed with a little sesame oil. Chicken is pounded after cooking, hence the name.

1. Place chicken and salt in a medium saucepan; add water to cover. Bring to a boil. Reduce heat; simmer 10 minutes.
2. Remove chicken; discard cooking liquid. With a rolling pin, pound cooked chicken until soft.
3. Place shredded lettuce on a serving dish. Shred chicken with your fingers; place on lettuce.
4. For sauce, in a small bowl, combine all sauce ingredients using chili sauce to taste. Pour sauce over chicken. Serve cold. Makes 4 servings.

芥 末 鷄 絲

Shredded Chicken in Mustard Sauce

2 tablespoons dry mustard
Water
2 boneless chicken breasts, shredded
1/2 teaspoon salt
2 egg whites, slightly beaten
1 tablespoon cornstarch
1/2 cup vegetable oil
1 tablespoon light soy sauce
1 tablespoon vinegar
2 teaspoons sesame oil

---

1. In a small bowl, blend dry mustard with enough cold water to form a thin paste. Let stand 30 minutes before using.
2. In a medium bowl, combine chicken, salt, egg whites and cornstarch.
3. Preheat a wok or large skillet over medium heat. Add vegetable oil. When hot, add chicken. Separate chicken shreds with chopsticks or a fork. Stir until chicken turns white. Remove chicken with a slotted spoon. Drain on paper towels. Arrange cooked chicken in a serving dish.
4. For sauce, in a small bowl, combine mustard mixture, soy sauce, vinegar and sesame oil. Pour sauce over chicken. Serve cold. Makes 4 servings.

Soya Duck

1 (4-1/2- to 5-lb.) duck
About 4 cups water
2 teaspoons salt
4 green onions
4 thin gingerroot slices
1 teaspoon five-spice powder
3 tablespoons rice wine or dry sherry
6 tablespoons dark soy sauce
2/3 cup packed brown sugar
1 tablespoon sesame oil

---

1. Remove and discard excess fat and tail from duck. Reserve giblets for Drunken Giblets, page 20, or another use.
2. In a large saucepan, bring water to a boil. Add duck; boil 1 minute. Remove duck from cooking liquid. Pat duck dry with paper towels. Rub 1 teaspoon salt inside duck.
3. Add remaining salt, onions, gingerroot and five-spice powder to cooking liquid remaining in saucepan. Bring to a boil.
4. Return duck to saucepan; add wine or sherry, soy sauce and sugar. Reduce heat. Cover; simmer duck 1-1/2 hours. Lift out duck; rub with sesame oil.
5. Boil cooking liquid until slightly reduced. Baste duck with reduced cooking liquid several times. Chop duck into small pieces, page 8. Serve hot or cold. Makes 4 servings.

醉 鴨 肫

Drunken Giblets

Giblets from 2 or 3 ducks or chickens
Water
2 tablespoons rice wine or dry sherry
1 tablespoon brandy
1 teaspoon salt
1 tablespoon sugar
1/2 cup chicken stock

To garnish:
1 teaspoon thinly shredded gingerroot

The neck, heart, wing tips, gizzard and liver are usually considered giblets. These are often discarded or used for making stock. However, giblets can make excellent dishes in their own right.

1. For this dish, use gizzards, hearts and livers. Remove and discard any fat.
2. Place giblets in a medium saucepan. Add cold water to cover. Bring to a boil over medium heat. Reduce heat; simmer 5 to 6 minutes. Remove giblets with a slotted spoon; discard cooking liquid. Cut giblets into thin slices.
3. In same saucepan, combine sliced giblets, wine or sherry, brandy, salt, sugar and stock. Bring to a boil; reduce heat. Simmer 10 minutes. Cool giblets in cooking liquid.
4. To serve, remove giblets with a slotted spoon; discard cooking liquid. Arrange on a serving plate; garnish with gingerroot. Makes 4 servings.

鹽 水 鴨

Salted Peking Duck

1 (4-1/2- to 5-lb.) duck
6 cups water
2 green onions
1 tablespoon Szechuan or black peppercorns
1 tablespoon salt
3 thin gingerroot slices
3 tablespoons rice wine or dry sherry

---

1. Remove and discard tail and excess fat from duck. Reserve giblets for Drunken Giblets, left, or another use. Place duck in a large saucepan; add water to cover. Bring to a boil over medium heat. Reduce heat. Cover; simmer duck 1 hour.
2. Remove duck from saucepan, reserving 1/2 cup liquid. Remove meat from bones.
3. In a medium saucepan, combine duck meat, onions, peppercorns, salt, gingerroot, wine or sherry and reserved cooking liquid.
4. Cover; cook over high heat 10 minutes. Remove from heat; let duck cool in cooking liquid.
5. To serve, remove duck from liquid; cut into thin slices or strips. Strain liquid; pour over duck. Serve cold. Makes 4 servings.

滷 肚 片

Braised Tripe

1-1/2 to 1-3/4 lbs. tripe
2 tablespoons vegetable oil
2 thin gingerroot slices
2 green onions
1 teaspoon five-spice powder
3 tablespoons rice wine or dry sherry
1/4 cup soy sauce
1 tablespoon sugar
4 cups chicken stock

To garnish:
2 teaspoons sesame oil
1 teaspoon finely chopped fresh coriander or
    green onion

---

1. Pat tripe dry with paper towels. Heat vegetable oil in a large heavy saucepan. Add tripe; sauté until browned. Add remaining ingredients; bring to a boil.
2. Reduce heat. Cover; simmer 1-1/4 hours.
3. Remove tripe from cooking liquid, discarding liquid. Cut cooked tripe into small pieces; place in a serving dish.
4. Garnish with sesame oil and coriander or onion. Serve cold as an appetizer or hot as a main-dish. Makes about 12 appetizers or 4 main dish servings.

炮腰花

Kidney Salad

2 lamb or veal kidneys
2 cups water
2 thin gingerroot slices, thinly shredded
Sauce:
1/2 teaspoon salt
2 tablespoons rice wine or dry sherry
1 tablespoon sesame oil
To garnish:
1 green onion, chopped

1. Remove and discard thin membrane covering kidneys. Split kidneys in half lengthwise. Discard fat and tough white core from center. Diagonally score surface of kidneys in a crisscross pattern. Cut into thin slices.
2. Pour water into a medium saucepan; bring to a boil over medium heat. Add kidney slices. Remove kidney slices as soon as water comes to a boil again. Drain kidney slices, discarding cooking liquid. Rinse kidney slices with cold water; drain. Place drained kidney slices in a serving dish.
3. Stir gingerroot into kidney slices. In a small bowl, combine ingredients for sauce. Pour over kidneys. Let stand 10 to 15 minutes. Garnish with onion. Serve cold. Makes 4 servings.

1/Remove thin outer membrane from kidneys, if necessary. Cut each kidney in half lengthways.

2/Discard white core from center of each kidney half. Score outside of each kidney half in a crisscross pattern by making deep diagonal cuts in opposite directions.

Top to bottom: Kidney Salad, Braised Tripe

酸辣白菜

Hot & Sour Cabbage

1 (1-lb.) cabbage
1 green bell pepper
1 red bell pepper
2 tablespoons soy sauce
2 tablespoons vinegar
2 tablespoons sugar
1 teaspoon salt
3 tablespoons vegetable oil
4 to 6 hot chilies
12 Szechuan or black peppercorns
1 tablespoon sesame oil

1. Thinly shred cabbage and green and red peppers.
2. For sauce, in a small bowl, combine soy sauce, vinegar, sugar and salt; set aside.
3. Preheat a wok or large skillet over high heat. Add vegetable oil. When oil is hot, add chilies and peppercorns. Stir-fry a few seconds. Add shredded cabbage and bell peppers; stir-fry 1 to 1-1/2 minutes. Add sauce mixture; stir until well blended. Place cabbage mixture in a serving dish. Discard chilies and peppercorns, if desired
4. Sprinkle cabbage mixture with sesame oil. Serve hot or cold. Makes 4 servings.

白切肉

Crystal-Boiled Pork with Dip Sauce

1 (1-1/2- to 1-3/4-lb.) boneless pork roast
Boiling water
Sauce:
1/4 cup soy sauce
1 tablespoon sesame oil
1 teaspoon finely chopped green onion
1 teaspoon finely chopped gingerroot
1/2 teaspoon finely chopped garlic
1 teaspoon chili sauce, if desired

1. Put pork in a large saucepan. Add water to cover. Bring to a boil, skimming off foam from top. Reduce heat. Cover; simmer pork 1 hour or until tender. Remove pork from cooking liquid; discard liquid. Let pork cool slightly.
2. Thinly slice pork across grain. Put any uneven pieces in center of a serving dish. Arrange even slices in 2 neat rows on sides. Neatly arrange remaining slices in center to resemble an arched bridge.
3. In a small bowl, combine sauce ingredients. Pour sauce over pork slices or serve separately as a dip sauce. Makes 4 to 6 servings.

五香滷牛肉

Spiced Beef

1-1/2 lbs. beef stew cubes
4 thin gingerroot slices
3 tablespoon rice wine or dry sherry
1 tablespoon brandy
Water
2 tablespoons vegetable oil
1/4 cup soy sauce
1 tablespoon sugar
1 teaspoon five-spice powder

1. In a large saucepan over medium heat, combine beef, gingerroot, wine or sherry and brandy. Add water to cover. Bring to a boil, skimming off foam from top. Reduce heat. Cover; simmer 45 minutes.
2. Remove beef with a slotted spoon, reserving cooking liquid. Pat beef dry with paper towels. Heat oil in a wok or large skillet over high heat. Add cooked beef; stir-fry until browned.
3. Add soy sauce, sugar, five-spice powder and about half of reserved cooking liquid to beef. Reduce heat. Cover; simmer 40 to 45 minutes or until beef is tender.
4. Remove beef from cooking liquid; thinly slice. Return beef to cooking liquid. Spoon beef mixture into a serving dish. Serve hot or cold. Makes 4 servings.

Clockwise from bottom: Hot & Sour Cabbage, Braised Bean Curd, Crystal-Boiled Pork with Dip Sauce

滷 豆 腐

Braised Bean Curd

1 lb. firm bean curd
Water
2 bacon slices or 2 oz. salt pork, blanched
2 green onions, cut into 1/2-inch lengths
2 thin gingerroot slices
1/3 cup soy sauce
3 tablespoons rice wine or dry sherry
2 tablespoons sugar

To garnish:
Parsley sprigs

1. If using 1 (1-lb.) bean-curd cake, cut in half lengthwise. Place bean curd in a saucepan; add water to cover. Bring to a boil. Add bacon or salt pork, onions, gingerroot, soy sauce, wine or sherry and sugar.
2. Reduce heat. Cover; simmer 20 minutes. Bean-curd texture will resemble a honeycomb.
3. Remove pan from heat; let cooked bean curd cool in cooking liquid.
4. Carefully remove bean curd with a slotted spoon, discarding cooking liquid and solid ingredients. Drain bean curd well. Cut bean curd into 1/4-inch slices; arrange on a platter. Garnish with parsley sprigs. Makes 4 to 6 servings.

茉 松

Crispy "Seaweed"

1-1/2 to 1-3/4 lbs. spinach or parsley
Vegetable oil for deep-frying
1 teaspoon salt
1-1/2 teaspoons sugar

The popular "seaweed" served in Chinese restaurants is, in fact, not seaweed! It is often spinach or parsley. Although real seaweed is eaten in China, this is an authentic recipe from Peking. This recipe is an ideal garnish for a number of dishes, particularly cold starters and buffet dishes.

1. Wash and dry spinach or parsley; shred with a sharp knife into thinnest possible shavings. Spread out on paper towels or put in a large colander 30 minutes to dry thoroughly.
2. Heat oil in a wok or deep-fryer over medium-high heat. Add shredded spinach or parsley in 2 to 3 batches. Stir with chopsticks until spinach or parsley starts to float to surface. Remove with a slotted spoon. Drain fried spinach or parsley on paper towels to remove as much oil as possible.
3. Place in a serving dish. Sprinkle with salt and sugar. Stir gently. Serve cold.

Variation
Deep-fry 2 ounces sliced almonds until crisp. Use as a garnish.

糖 醋 黄 瓜

Sweet & Sour Cucumber

1 cucumber
1 teaspoon salt
2 tablespoons sugar
2 tablespoons vinegar

Select a dark-green cucumber that is young and tender. Seeds will be smaller and more tender, and cucumber will be less bitter.

1. Split cucumber in half lengthways. Cut halves into strips. In a medium bowl, sprinkle cucumber strips with salt. Let stand 10 minutes to extract bitter juices.
2. Remove salted cucumber strips from bowl; rinse with cold water, if desired. Pat dry with paper towels.
3. Place cucumber strips on a serving dish. Sprinkle with sugar and then vinegar. Makes 4 servings.

Left to right: Crispy "Seaweed" with Almonds, Sweet & Sour Cucumber

三色拼盘

Assorted Hors d'Oeuvres (1)

1/2 recipe Rapid-Fried Shrimp in Shells, page 14
1/2 recipe Szechuan Bang-Bang Chicken, page 19,
   without lettuce
1/4 recipe Spiced Beef, page 22, thinly sliced

To garnish:
Crispy "Seaweed," page 24, or 1/2 cucumber,
   thinly sliced

At the start of a meal, serve a selection of thinly sliced cooked meats instead of several different dishes. Neatly arrange meats on a large plate with some colorful garnishes. This assorted hors d'oeuvre consists of three basic ingredients: fish, chicken and meat. Similar foods can be substituted if the Chinese principles of harmony, contrast and balance, both in color and flavor, are followed.

1. Neatly arrange each ingredient in separate rows on a serving plate. Garnish with either "Seaweed" or cucumber slices.
2. All cooking can be done in advance. To avoid a last-minute rush, arrange meats and garnish plate before guests arrive. Makes 8 to 10 servings.

什 錦 冷 盤

Assorted Hors d'Oeuvres (2)

This is a more elaborate version of previous recipe, page 25. Again, ingredients are chosen for harmonious contrast and balance in color, flavor and texture. Because large numbers of different ingredients are used in this recipe, quantities of each item are not given. It can be adapted to suit the occasion. As a guide, 2 ounces of each item should serve 8 to 10 people.

Here is a suggestion list. Other recipes can be substituted to create original variations. Do not have more than one of the same type of dish.

1. Hot Mixed Shrimp, page 14
2. Shanghai "Smoked" Fish, page 16
3. Shredded Chicken in Mustard Sauce, page 19
4. Soya Duck, page 19
5. Braised Tripe, page 20
6. Crystal-Boiled Pork, page 22
7. Braised Bean Curd, page 23
8. Sweet & Sour Cucumber, page 24

To garnish:
Tomatoes, green onions, radishes or lettuce

To make radish garnishes, choose large smooth radishes. Using a sharp knife, make several cuts on each radish about two-thirds of the way but not all the way through. Radishes can be placed on a cutting board between 2 chopsticks for cutting. Chopsticks will stop the knife from cutting all the way through radish. Place cut radishes in a large jar. Add 1/2 teaspoon salt and 1-1/2 teaspoons sugar; shake jar to coat each radish. Seal and refrigerate several hours or overnight. Before serving, pour off accumulated liquid; spread out each radish like a fan.

To make green-onion flowers, trim both ends so stalk measures about 3 inches. Use a sharp knife to shred green tops to within 1 inch of white stem. Put onions into ice-cold water 1 hour. Drain; pat dry with paper towels before using. Onions can remain in water several hours.

Top plate: Left: Shanghai "Smoked Fish"; Center: Soya Duck; Right: Crystal-Boiled Pork

Bottom plate: Outside ring from left: Sweet & Sour Cucumbers, Braised Bean Curd, Shanghai "Smoked Fish," Crystal-Boiled Pork; Inner area from left: Hot Mixed Shrimp, Shredded Chicken in Mustard Sauce, Braised Tripe

Soups

清 湯

Basic Stock for Soups

1 (3- to 4-lb.) stewing chicken or 3 lbs. pork spareribs
11 cups water
4 to 6 thin gingerroot slices
3 or 4 green onions

1. Place all ingredients in a large saucepan. Bring to a boil, skimming off any foam from top. Reduce heat. Cover; simmer 2 to 2-1/2 hours.
2. Strain stock when slightly cooled; refrigerate. Discard chicken or spareribs; no flavor remains in them. Discard gingerroot and onions.
3. Lift fat from top of cold stock before using. Stock will keep in refrigerator 3 or 4 days. Freeze if storing for a longer period. Makes 7 to 8 cups.

白 菜 肉 片 湯

Sliced Pork & Cabbage Soup

4 oz. lean pork
1 tablespoon rice wine or dry sherry
1 tablespoon soy sauce
1/2 medium Chinese cabbage
2 cups Basic Stock, above, using chicken
1 teaspoon salt

1. Thinly slice pork. In a medium bowl, combine wine or sherry and soy sauce. Add sliced pork; let stand 10 minutes.
2. Cut cabbage in 1-inch lengths.
3. In a medium saucepan, bring stock to a boil. Add seasoned pork, stirring to keep slices separate. Boil 30 seconds; add sliced cabbage and salt. Reduce heat; simmer 1-1/2 to 2 minutes. Cabbage should remain crisp. Makes 4 servings.

Left to right: Sliced Pork & Cabbage Soup, Chinese Mushroom Soup
On chopping block with cleaver, left to right: gingerroot, shredded cabbage, sliced gingerroot, dried Chinese mushrooms

冬 菇 湯

Chinese Mushroom Soup

6 medium dried Chinese mushrooms or
   4 oz. fresh mushrooms
2 teaspoons cornstarch
1 tablespoon cold water
3 egg whites
2 teaspoons salt
2 cups Basic Stock, opposite

To garnish:
1 teaspoon finely chopped green onion

1. Soak dried mushrooms in warm water 20 minutes or until softened. Rinse; squeeze dry. Discard hard stems; cut caps into thin slices. If using fresh mushrooms, wipe with damp paper towels; thinly slice.
2. In a small bowl, combine cornstarch and cold water; set aside. Stir egg whites with a fork to blend; do not froth. Add a pinch of salt.
3. In a medium saucepan, bring stock to a boil; add sliced mushrooms. Boil 1 minute. Stir in cornstarch mixture; stir constantly until thickened.
4. Add remaining salt. Slowly pour egg whites into soup, stirring constantly. Cook 1 minute.
5. Serve hot. Garnish with onion. Makes 4 servings.

蛋 花 湯

Egg-Drop Soup

2 eggs
1 teaspoon salt
2 cups Basic Stock, opposite
2 teaspoons finely chopped green onion

1. In a small bowl, beat eggs with a pinch of salt; set aside.
2. In a medium saucepan, bring stock to a boil. Slowly pour beaten eggs into boiling stock, stirring constantly. Cook 1 minute.
3. Place remaining salt and onions in a serving bowl. Add soup; serve hot. Makes 4 servings.

一品豆腐湯
Bean-Curd Soup

8 oz. bean curd
4 oz. fresh, frozen or canned crabmeat
1 bunch watercress
2 cups Basic Stock, page 28
1 teaspoon salt

1. Cut bean-curd cake into 40 small cubes.
2. Flake crabmeat into small pieces. Wash watercress; coarsely chop.
3. In a medium saucepan, bring stock to a boil; add salt, bean-curd cubes and crabmeat pieces. Boil 1 minute.
4. Place chopped watercress in a large serving bowl. Add soup; stir. Serve hot. Makes 4 servings.

氽肝片湯
Liver Soup

4 oz. calves' liver
1 teaspoon cornstarch
4 oz. spinach leaves
2 cups Basic Stock, page 28
1 teaspoon salt
1 tablespoon soy sauce
1 teaspoon sesame oil

1. Thinly slice liver; cut slices into 1-inch pieces. In a medium bowl, combine liver and cornstarch; toss to coat.
2. Wash spinach; cut large leaves into 2 or 3 pieces.
3. In a medium saucepan, bring stock to a boil; add coated liver, spinach pieces, salt and soy sauce. Boil 1 minute.
4. Add sesame oil. Serve hot. Makes 4 servings.

魚片湯
Sliced Fish Soup

8 oz. white fish
1 egg white
1 tablespoon cornstarch
1 small head lettuce
2 cups Basic Stock, page 28
Salt
Freshly ground white pepper

To garnish:
1 tablespoon finely chopped green onion

---

1. Cut fish into 2-inch slices. In a medium bowl, combine fish slices, egg white and cornstarch. Thinly shred lettuce.
2. In a medium saucepan, bring stock to a boil. Add salt and fish slices. Cook 1 minute.
3. Place shredded lettuce in a large serving bowl; season with white pepper. Add soup to bowl; garnish with onion. Serve hot. Makes 4 servings.

魚丸湯
Fish Balls with Vegetable Soup

2 oz. mushrooms
2 oz. cooked ham
2 oz. bamboo shoots
2 cups Basic Stock, page 28
4 oz. fish balls, see below
Salt

To garnish:
Chopped fresh coriander leaves

Fish balls can be bought in Oriental stores or made at home. To make fish balls, mince 4 ounces fresh fish, such as cod or haddock. With an electric mixer, beat minced fish, 1 egg, 1 tablespoon cornstarch and a few drops of vegetable oil 5 to 10 minutes or until fluffy. Or, mince fish in a food processor fitted with a steel blade; add remaining ingredients. Process until mixture is blended and fluffy. Chill mixture 1 hour or until firm; shape into walnut-size balls.

1. Thinly slice mushrooms, ham and bamboo shoots.
2. In a medium saucepan, bring stock to a boil. Add fish balls, one at a time. When fish balls float to surface of stock, add sliced mushrooms, ham, bamboo shoots and salt. Cook 1 minute.
3. Spoon soup into a serving bowl; top with coriander. Serve hot. Makes 4 servings.

The Chinese traditionally make marvelous soups merely by stir-frying a handful of fresh greens or whatever is at hand. Water and seasoning are added and the mixture is brought to a rapid boil. If some ready-made stock is available, there is no limit to what can be made into an instantly prepared soup. In China, the very best stock is made from a whole chicken, a whole duck and a leg of lamb or pork. Of course, a perfectly good stock can be made by following the recipe on page 28.

A chicken bouillon cube dissolved in hot water or canned bouillon or broth can be substituted for home-made stock, but the flavor will not be as good. Commercial products are salted, while Basic Stock is not, so adjust seasoning accordingly.

Left to right: Liver Soup, Sliced Fish Soup, Fish Balls with Vegetable Soup

三鮮湯

Three-Flavors (Pork, Chicken & Shrimp) Soup

---

4 oz. lean pork
4 oz. boneless chicken breast, skinned
4 oz. peeled, deveined uncooked shrimp
2 cups Basic Stock, page 28
About 1 teaspoon salt

---

1. Thinly slice pork and chicken. Cut slices into small pieces. If shrimp are large, cut into 2 or 3 pieces.
2. In a medium saucepan, bring stock to a boil. Add pork, chicken, shrimp and salt. Cook 1-1/2 minutes.
3. Ladle into 4 individual soup bowls. Season with salt. Serve hot. Makes 4 servings.

Variation
Substitute scallops, crab, lobster, oysters or abalone for shrimp.

雞絲火腿湯

Chicken & Ham Soup

---

4 oz. boneless chicken breast, skinned
4 oz. cooked ham
2 cups Basic Stock, page 28
Salt

To garnish:
1 teaspoon finely chopped green onion

---

1. Thinly slice chicken and ham; cut slices into small pieces.
2. In a medium saucepan, bring stock to a boil. Add sliced chicken, ham and salt. Cook 1 minute.
3. Place onion in a serving bowl; add soup. Serve hot. Makes 4 servings.

羊肉黃瓜湯

Lamb & Cucumber Soup

---

8 oz. lean lamb
1 tablespoon rice wine or dry sherry
1 tablespoon soy sauce
1/2 medium cucumber
2 cups Basic Stock, page 28
Salt

To garnish:
1 teaspoon finely chopped green onion

---

1. Thinly slice lamb; cut slices into 1-inch pieces. In a medium saucepan, combine wine or sherry, soy sauce and lamb slices. Let stand 10 minutes.
2. Thinly slice unpeeled cucumber.
3. In a medium saucepan, bring stock to a boil. Add seasoned lamb, sliced cucumber and salt; stir to separate. Cook 1-1/2 to 2 minutes or until lamb is cooked.
4. Place onion in a serving bowl; add soup. Serve hot. Makes 4 servings.

Left to right: Chicken & Ham Soup, Lamb & Cucumber Soup, Eight-Treasure Soup

Eight-Treasure Soup

2 oz. peeled, deveined uncooked shrimp or
   1 tablespoon dried shrimp
2 oz. boneless chicken breast, skinned
2 oz. lean pork
2 oz. bamboo shoots
4 oz. bean curd
2 medium tomatoes, peeled
1 egg
Salt
1 tablespoon cornstarch
1 tablespoon water
2-1/2 cups Basic Stock, page 28
3/4 cup shredded spinach leaves
1 tablespoon soy sauce
Freshly ground pepper

To garnish:
1 tablespoon finely chopped green onion

This soup is for special occasions, such as a New Year's Feast or birthday celebration. If color and textures are considered, ingredients can be varied according to the season.

1. If using dried shrimp, soak in warm water 20 minutes; drain. If using fresh shrimp, cut into 3 to 4 pieces. Thinly shred chicken, pork, bamboo shoots, bean curd and tomatoes. Beat egg with a pinch of salt. In a small bowl, combine cornstarch and water.

2. In a medium saucepan, bring stock to a boil. Add chopped or soaked shrimp and shredded chicken and pork. When shrimp, chicken and pork rise to surface of stock, slowly pour in beaten egg, stirring constantly. Add spinach, shredded bean curd and tomatoes and soy sauce. Cook 1 minute.

3. Stir cornstarch mixture into hot soup. Cook until thickened, stirring constantly. Season with salt and pepper. Garnish with onion. Serve hot. Makes 4 to 6 servings.

甜 酸 排 骨

Pork Spareribs in Cantonese Sweet & Sour Sauce

1-1/2 lbs. pork spareribs
1/2 teaspoon salt
Freshly ground Szechuan or black pepper
1 teaspoon sugar
1 tablespoon cornstarch
1 egg yolk
Vegetable oil for deep-frying
2 tablespoons all-purpose flour
1 small green bell pepper, shredded
1 small red bell pepper, shredded
1 tablespoon soy sauce
3 tablespoons sugar
3 tablespoons vinegar
1 tablespoon cornstarch blended with
   3 tablespoons water

The sauce is bright and translucent, not too sweet or too sour, and the meat is succulent.

1. Cut spareribs into individual ribs. With a cleaver, chop each rib into 2 or 3 pieces. In a large bowl, combine chopped spareribs, salt, pepper, sugar and cornstarch. Stir in egg yolk until distributed. Let stand 10 minutes.
2. Heat oil in a wok or deep saucepan over medium heat. Coat each sparerib piece with flour before deep-frying. Add coated sparerib pieces to hot oil, one at a time. Separate with chopsticks, if necessary. Deep-fry until crisp and golden; remove spareribs with a slotted spoon.
3. Heat oil until bubbling. Add deep-fried spareribs; deep-fry again 30 seconds or until golden brown. Remove with a slotted spoon or strainer; drain on paper towels.
4. Pour off oil, leaving about 1 tablespoon in wok or saucepan. Place wok or saucepan over high heat. When oil is hot, add bell peppers; stir-fry 30 seconds. Add soy sauce, sugar and vinegar. Stir a few times. Stir in cornstarch mixture. Stirring constantly, cook until sauce thickens; add spareribs. Stir well; serve immediately. Makes 4 servings.

滑 溜 里 脊 片

Pork Slices with Chinese Vegetables

8 oz. lean pork
1 tablespoon soy sauce
1 tablespoon rice wine or dry sherry
1 tablespoon cornstarch
Water
1/2 oz. wood ears
4 oz. Chinese pea pods, trimmed, or broccoli flowerets
1/4 cup vegetable oil
2 green onions, cut into 1-inch lengths
4 oz. bamboo shoots, sliced
4 oz. water chestnuts, sliced
1 teaspoon salt
1 teaspoon sugar
1 teaspoon sesame oil

---

1. Cut pork into small, thin slices. In a medium bowl, combine sliced pork, soy sauce, wine or sherry and 1/2 tablespoon cornstarch. In a small bowl, combine remaining cornstarch with a little water to make a paste; set aside.
2. Soak wood ears in warm water 15 to 20 minutes or until softened; rinse. Discard any hard parts. Coarsely chop. If pea pods are large, cut in half. If using broccoli, cut flowerets into small pieces.
3. Preheat a wok or large skillet over high heat. Add vegetable oil. When hot, add seasoned pork; stir-fry 1 minute or until color changes. Remove pork with a slotted spoon.
4. To oil remaining in wok or skillet, add onions and pea pods or broccoli. Stir-fry 2 minutes. Stir in bamboo shoots, chopped wood ears, water chestnuts, salt and sugar. Add cooked pork; stir-fry 1 minute. Stir in cornstarch mixture; stirring constantly, cook until thickened. Stir in sesame oil; serve hot. Makes 4 servings.

Top to bottom: Pork Slices with Chinese Vegetables, Pork Spareribs in Cantonese Sweet & Sour Sauce

豉椒牛肉

Beef & Green Peppers in Cantonese Black-Bean Sauce

1 (8- to 10-oz.) beef-flank steak
1/4 teaspoon salt
1 tablespoon soy sauce
1 tablespoon rice wine or dry sherry
1 teaspoon sugar
1 tablespoon cornstarch
1 small green bell pepper
1 medium onion
1/4 cup vegetable oil
2 teaspoons shredded gingerroot
2 green onions, shredded
1 or 2 green or red chilies, shredded
1-1/2 tablespoons fermented black beans crushed in
   1 tablespoon rice wine or dry sherry

Although pork is the most popular meat in China, beef is an important part of the diet of Chinese Moslems. There are about four million Chinese Moslems widely distributed throughout China.

1. Cut beef into thin slices about 1-1/2 inches across. In a medium bowl, combine sliced beef, salt, soy sauce, wine or sherry, sugar and cornstarch.
2. Slice green pepper and onion into 1-inch squares.
3. Preheat a wok or large skillet over high heat. Add oil. When oil smokes, add seasoned beef; stir-fry a few seconds. Remove beef with a slotted spoon. To same oil, add gingerroot, green onions, chilies and green-pepper and onion squares; stir-fry a few seconds. Add crushed black-bean mixture and cooked beef. Stir-fry 1 minute. Serve immediately. Makes 4 servings.

Variation
Substitute purchased black-bean sauce for black-bean-and-wine mixture. Flavor will be slightly different.

干炒牛肉絲

Szechuan Dry-Fried Shredded Beef

2 tablespoons sesame oil
1 (10-oz.) beef-flank steak, shredded
2 tablespoons rice wine or dry sherry
1 tablespoon hot bean paste
1 tablespoon Hoisin sauce or barbecue sauce
1 garlic clove, finely chopped
1/2 teaspoon salt
1 tablespoon sugar
2 carrots, shredded
2 green onions, finely chopped
2 teaspoons finely chopped gingerroot
1/2 teaspoon freshly ground Szechuan or black pepper
1 teaspoon chili oil

Dry-frying is a cooking method unique to Szechuan cuisine. Main ingredients are slowly stir-fried over low heat with any seasonings. Additional ingredients are added, and the mixture quickly stir-fried over high heat.

1. Heat a wok or skillet over high heat. Add sesame oil. When hot, add beef with 1 tablespoon wine or sherry; stir-fry until beef shreds separate.
2. Reduce heat. Pour off excess liquid; stir gently until beef is completely dry. Stir in bean paste, Hoisin or barbecue sauce, garlic, salt, sugar and remaining wine or sherry. Stir a few times.
3. Increase heat to high. Add carrots; stir-fry 1 minute. Add onions, gingerroot, pepper and chili oil; stir-fry 1 minute. Serve hot. Makes 4 servings.

Variation
Substitute 3 or 4 shredded celery stalks for carrots, or use half carrots and half celery.

Clockwise from top: Cantonese Beef in Oyster Sauce, Beef & Green Peppers in Cantonese Black-Bean Sauce, Szechuan Dry-Fried Shredded Beef

蠔油牛肉

Cantonese Beef in Oyster Sauce

1 (8- to-10 oz.) beef-flank steak
Salt
1/2 teaspoon freshly ground pepper
1 teaspoon sugar
1 tablespoon light soy sauce
2 tablespoons rice wine or dry sherry
1 tablespoon cornstarch
1 egg
1 small Chinese cabbage
1/4 cup vegetable oil
1 green onion, finely chopped
2 teaspoons finely chopped gingerroot
1-1/2 tablespoons oyster sauce

1. Cut beef into thin slices about 1-1/2 inches across. In a medium bowl, combine sliced beef, a pinch of salt, pepper, sugar, soy sauce, wine or sherry, cornstarch and egg. Let stand 20 to 30 minutes.
2. Cut each Chinese-cabbage leaf into 2 or 3 pieces.
3. Preheat a wok or large skillet over high heat. Add 2 tablespoons oil. When oil smokes, add cabbage pieces; stir-fry 1-1/2 to 2 minutes or until leaves become limp. Quickly remove with a slotted spoon; place cabbage in a serving dish.
4. Wash and dry wok or skillet. Add remaining oil. When oil smokes, add onion and gingerroot; stir-fry a few seconds. Add seasoned beef; stir-fry 1 minute. Add oyster sauce; stir-fry 1 minute. Spoon beef mixture over cabbage. Makes 4 servings.

青椒炒鷄絲

Shredded Chicken Breast with Green Peppers

2 boneless chicken-breast halves, shredded
1 teaspoon salt
1 egg white
1 tablespoon cornstarch
Water
1/4 cup vegetable oil
1 green onion, finely chopped
2 teaspoons finely chopped gingerroot
1 large green bell pepper, shredded
2 tablespoons rice wine or dry sherry
1 teaspoon sesame oil

Do not overcook this dish. When correctly done, chicken should be tender and peppers should be crunchy and shining.

1. In a medium bowl, combine chicken and 1/2 teaspoon salt. Stir in egg white; then stir in 2 teaspoons cornstarch. In a small bowl, combine remaining cornstarch and a little water to make a paste; set aside.
2. Preheat a wok or large skillet over medium heat. Add vegetable oil. When oil is warm, add coated chicken; stir-fry until white. See box, below. Remove chicken with a slotted spoon.
3. Increase heat to high. When oil is very hot, add onion and gingerroot. Stir-fry a few seconds. Add green peppers; stir-fry 30 seconds. Add cooked chicken, remaining salt and wine or sherry. Stir 30 seconds. Stir in cornstarch mixture; cook until thickened. Stir in sesame oil. Serve hot. Makes 4 servings.

辣子鷄丁

Chicken Cubes with Walnuts Szechuan-Style

8 to 10 oz. boneless chicken, cut into 1/2-inch cubes
1/2 teaspoon salt
1 egg white
1 tablespoon cornstarch
1/4 cup vegetable oil
2 green onions, finely chopped
2 teaspoons finely chopped gingerroot
1/2 cup coarsely chopped walnuts
1 tablespoon crushed yellow-bean sauce
1 green bell pepper, cut into 1-inch pieces
2 teaspoons sugar
2 tablespoons rice wine or dry sherry
About 1 tablespoon chili sauce
2 teaspoons cornstarch blended with 1 tablespoon water

---

1. In a medium bowl, combine chicken and salt. Stir in egg white; then stir in cornstarch.
2. Preheat a wok or large skillet over medium heat. Add oil. When oil is warm, add coated chicken; stir-fry 10 seconds. Remove chicken with a slotted spoon.
3. Increase heat to high. When oil is hot, add onions, gingerroot and walnuts; stir-fry a few seconds. Add bean sauce; stir-fry a few seconds. Add green pepper and cooked chicken; stir-fry a few seconds. Add sugar, wine or sherry and chili sauce, to taste; stir-fry 30 seconds. Stir in cornstarch mixture; stirring constantly, cook until thickened. Serve hot. Makes 4 servings.

Variation
Substitute almonds, cashews or peanuts for walnuts.

Combining chicken with salt, egg white and corn-starch prior to cooking is a technique known as *velveting*. The coating forms a barrier between the chicken and hot oil. This preserves chicken's natural delicate texture. Oil should not be too hot (about 325F, 165C) in the first cooking stage; use medium heat. The second cooking is done over high heat. Fresh rather than frozen chicken is preferred.

Clockwise from top: Chicken Cubes with Walnuts Szechuan-Style, Shredded Chicken Breast with Green Peppers, Cooked Rice

醬爆鷄脯丁

Diced Chicken in Peking Bean Sauce

1 egg white
1 tablespoon cornstarch
Water
Vegetable oil for deep-frying
2 boneless chicken breasts, cut into 1/2-inch cubes
2 tablespoons crushed yellow-bean sauce
1 tablespoon sugar
1 tablespoon rice wine or dry sherry
1 teaspoon sesame oil

1. In a shallow bowl, lightly beat egg white. In a small bowl, blend cornstarch and 2 tablespoons water into a smooth paste.
2. Heat vegetable oil in a wok or deep saucepan over medium heat until warm. Dip chicken cubes in egg white, then in cornstarch mixture. Gently drop coated chicken into warm oil; see box, opposite page. Deep-fry over medium heat a few seconds. Remove chicken with a slotted spoon; drain on paper towels.
3. Pour off all oil. Place wok or saucepan over high heat. Add bean sauce; stir a few times. Add sugar; stir until sugar dissolves. Add wine or sherry and sesame oil; stir constantly until well blended. Add 1 tablespoon water, if necessary. Add drained chicken; stir until coated with sauce.
4. Serve hot. Makes 4 servings.

Left to right: Mu-Shu Pork Shandong-Style, Pork with Szechuan Preserved Vegetable

椒盐排骨

Szechuan Fried Pork Spareribs

1 lb. pork spareribs
1 teaspoon salt
1 teaspoon freshly ground Szechuan or black pepper
1/2 teaspoon five-spice powder
2 tablespoons rice wine or dry sherry
1 egg
2 tablespoons cornstarch
Vegetable oil for deep-frying

Dip:
2 teaspoons salt
2 teaspoons freshly ground Szechuan or black pepper

1. With a cleaver, chop each rib into 2 or 3 pieces. In a large bowl, combine chopped spareribs, salt, pepper, five-spice powder and wine or sherry. Let stand 15 minutes.
2. In a large bowl, beat egg with cornstarch to make a smooth batter. Stir in seasoned spareribs.
3. Heat oil in a wok or deep-fryer. Add coated spareribs; deep-fry until golden. Remove spareribs with a slotted spoon. Reheat oil. Add cooked spareribs; deep-fry once more to crisp them.
4. To make dip, combine salt and pepper. Serve hot cooked spareribs with salt and pepper dip. Makes 4 servings.

回鍋肉

Pork with Szechuan Preserved Vegetable

8 to 10 oz. pork, in 1 piece
Boiling water
4 oz. Szechuan preserved vegetable, see box below
3 tablespoons vegetable oil
4 oz. broccoli flowerets
2 green onions, finely chopped
2 teaspoons finely chopped gingerroot
1 garlic clove, finely chopped
1 tablespoon rice wine or dry sherry
1 tablespoon hot bean paste
1 teaspoon cornstarch mixed with 1 tablespoon water

This traditional Szechuan dish is also known as Twice-Cooked Pork. The chilies in the bean paste make it hot. To reduce hotness, substitute sweet bean paste for hot bean paste or reduce amount of Szechuan preserved vegetable.

1. Place pork in a large saucepan. Add boiling water to cover. Simmer 20 to 25 minutes. Remove pork. Cool slightly; cut into thin slices 1-1/2 inches across; reserve.
2. Cut Szechuan preserved vegetable slices same size as pork.
3. Preheat a wok or large skillet over high heat. Add oil. When oil is hot, add sliced preserved vegetable and broccoli; stir-fry 1 minute. Add sliced pork, onions, gingerroot, garlic, wine or sherry and bean paste; stir-fry 1 minute. Stir in cornstarch mixture; cook until thickened. Serve hot. Makes 4 servings.

The appearance of Szechuan preserved vegetable is somewhat forbidding. It is covered by a thick, red paste that has a strong odor. Szechuan preserved vegetable is crunchy with a refreshing salty aftertaste. Before using preserved vegetable, wash in cold water to remove paste. Rub knobby contours to clean them thoroughly. Store unwashed knobs in an airtight jar in the refrigerator. They will keep indefinitely.

木樨肉

Mu-Shu Pork Shandong-Style

1/4 oz. wood ears
3 eggs
1 teaspoon salt
1/4 cup vegetable oil
6 to 8 oz. lean pork, shredded
8 oz. Chinese cabbage, shredded
2 green onions, cut into 2-inch lengths
1 tablespoon light soy sauce
1 tablespoon rice wine or dry sherry

Mu-shu is the Chinese name for cassia, a fragrant yellow flower that blooms in early autumn. In China, egg dishes with bright yellow color are often given the name Mu-shu. To follow tradition, eat this dish as a filling for Thin Pancakes, page 76. If desired, serve with rice or as a hot starter.

1. Soak wood ears in water 20 minutes or until softened. Remove any hard parts. Rinse; thinly shred.
2. Lightly beat eggs with a pinch of salt. Heat 1 tablespoon oil in a wok or skillet over medium heat. When oil is hot, pour in beaten eggs. Stir eggs until lightly set. Remove eggs; set aside.
3. Wash and dry wok or skillet. Add remaining oil. Heat over high heat. When oil is hot, add pork; stir-fry 30 seconds. Add cabbage, shredded wood ears and onions; stir-fry 30 seconds. Add remaining salt, soy sauce and wine or sherry. Stir-fry 1 to 1-1/2 minutes. Add cooked eggs; stir to break eggs into shreds. Stir until blended. Makes 4 servings.

Variation
Substitute bamboo shoots, celery or bean sprouts for cabbage. Do not use canned bean sprouts. They do not have the crispness of fresh sprouts. Substitute fresh mushrooms for wood ears, if desired.

葱爆羊肉

Rapid-Fried Lamb Slices

8 to 10 oz. lean lamb
About 12 green onions
1/4 cup vegetable oil
1 tablespoon soy sauce
1/2 teaspoon salt
1 tablespoon rice wine or dry sherry
1/2 teaspoon freshly ground Szechuan or black pepper
2 teaspoons cornstarch
1 garlic clove, crushed
1 tablespoon sesame oil
1 tablespoon vinegar

This dish must be cooked over highest heat in shortest possible time, otherwise meat will not be tender and juicy.

1. Trim and discard fat from lamb. Slice lamb as thinly as possible. Cut onions in half lengthwise; slice diagonally.
2. In a medium bowl, combine sliced lamb, sliced onions, 1 tablespoon vegetable oil, soy sauce, salt, wine or sherry, pepper and cornstarch.
3. Preheat a wok or large skillet over high heat. Add remaining vegetable oil. When oil smokes, add garlic; stir-fry a few seconds. Add seasoned lamb and onions; stir-fry a few seconds. Add sesame oil and vinegar; stir briefly. Serve hot. Makes 4 servings.

火爆猪干

Fried Liver Szechuan-Style

8 oz. calves' liver
1 tablespoon cornstarch
Water
1/2 teaspoon salt
1/2 teaspoon freshly ground Szechuan or black pepper
2 tablespoons rice wine or dry sherry
1/4 cup vegetable oil
2 green onions, finely chopped
2 teaspoons finely chopped gingerroot
6 oz. bamboo shoots, sliced
1 garlic clove, finely chopped
1-1/2 tablespoons soy sauce
1 teaspoon sugar
1 teaspoon sesame oil

1. Cut liver into 1-1/2-inch pieces. In a medium bowl, combine 2 teaspoons cornstarch with a little water. Stir in liver pieces, salt, pepper and 1 tablespoon wine or sherry.
2. In a small bowl, combine remaining cornstarch and a little water to make a paste; set aside.
3. Preheat a wok or large skillet over high heat. Add vegetable oil. When oil smokes, add seasoned liver. Stir to separate pieces. Stir-fry a few seconds. Remove with a slotted spoon. Liver is cooked quickly to retain its tenderness.
4. To same wok or skillet, add onions, gingerroot and bamboo shoots; stir-fry a few seconds. Add cooked liver, garlic, remaining wine or sherry, soy sauce, sugar and sesame oil. Stir to blend. Stir in cornstarch mixture; stirring constantly, cook until thickened. Serve hot. Makes 4 servings.

Variation
Substitute wood ears for bamboo shoots. Soak wood ears 20 minutes; discard any hard parts. Rinse, thinly slice. If desired, use a combination of bamboo shoots and wood ears.

醋溜腰花

Stir-Fried Kidney Flowers Shandong-Style

1/4 oz. wood ears
4 oz. cabbage, spinach or bok choy, coarsely chopped
Boiling water
2 veal kidneys or lamb kidneys
1 teaspoon salt
1 tablespoon cornstarch
3 tablespoons Basic Stock, page 28, or water
Vegetable oil for deep-frying
1 green onion, finely chopped
1 teaspoon finely chopped gingerroot
1 garlic clove, finely chopped
2 oz. bamboo shoots, sliced
2 oz. water chestnuts, sliced
1 tablespoon rice wine or dry sherry
1 tablespoon vinegar
1-1/2 tablespoons soy sauce
1 teaspoon sesame oil

This is a colorful and delicious dish. Even people who normally do not like kidneys enjoy this recipe.

1. Soak wood ears in water 15 to 20 minutes. Rinse; discard any hard parts. Cut each wood ear into 2 or 3 pieces. Blanch cabbage, spinach or bok choy briefly in boiling water.
2. Split each kidney in half lengthwise; discard white core from center. Diagonally score surface of each kidney half in a crisscross pattern, see page 21; cut each half into 6 to 8 pieces. In a medium bowl, combine scored kidney pieces, 1/2 teaspoon salt and 1/2 tablespoon cornstarch. In a small bowl, combine remaining cornstarch and stock or water; set aside.
3. Heat vegetable oil in a wok or deep saucepan over high heat. While oil is heating, pour boiling water over seasoned kidneys to blanch. Drain kidney pieces; pat dry with paper towels. When oil is hot, add blanched kidney pieces; deep-fry a few seconds. Remove kidneys with a slotted spoon.
4. Pour off oil, leaving 1 tablespoon in wok or skillet. Add onion, gingerroot and garlic; stir-fry a few seconds. Add soaked wood ears, bamboo shoots, water chestnuts, cooked kidney pieces, remaining salt, wine or sherry, vinegar, soy sauce and sesame oil; stir-fry 1 minute. Stir in cornstarch mixture; stirring constantly, cook until thickened. Serve hot. Makes 4 servings.

Left to right: Stir-Fried Kidney Flowers Shandong-Style, Rapid-Fried Lamb Slices

Chicken Breast & Egg White

2 boneless chicken-breast halves, sliced
1 teaspoon salt
2 egg whites
1 tablespoon cornstarch
1/4 cup vegetable oil
Shredded lettuce
1 teaspoon finely chopped gingerroot
1 green onion, finely chopped
4 oz. green peas
1 tablespoon rice wine or dry sherry
1 teaspoon sesame oil

1. In a medium bowl, combine chicken and 1/2 teaspoon salt. Stir in egg whites; then stir in cornstarch.
2. Preheat a wok or large skillet over medium heat. Add vegetable oil. When oil is warm, add coated chicken; stir-fry 30 seconds or until chicken turns white. See box, page 38. Remove chicken with a slotted spoon.
3. Increase heat to high. Add lettuce leaves and 1/2 teaspoon salt; stir-fry until lettuce is limp. With a slotted spoon, place lettuce in a serving dish.
4. Add gingerroot and onion to wok or skillet; stir-fry a few seconds. Add cooked chicken and peas; stir to blend. Add wine or sherry; stir-fry 30 seconds. Stir in sesame oil; serve chicken mixture over stir-fried lettuce leaves. Makes 4 servings.

Chicken Cubes with Celery

2 boneless chicken-breast halves, cut into
    1/2-inch cubes
1/2 teaspoon salt
1 egg white
1 tablespoon cornstarch
Water
3 or 4 celery stalks
1/4 cup vegetable oil
1 tablespoon rice wine or dry sherry
1 tablespoon light soy sauce

1. In a medium bowl, combine chicken and salt. stir in egg white; then stir in 1/2 tablespoon cornstarch. In a small bowl, combine remaining cornstarch and a little water to make a paste; set aside.
2. Diagonally cut celery stalks into 1/2-inch slices.
3. Preheat a wok or large skillet. Add oil. When oil is warm, add coated chicken; stir-fry 30 seconds or until chicken turns white. See box, page 38. Remove chicken with a slotted spoon.
4. Increase heat; when oil is very hot, add sliced celery. Stir-fry 1 minute. Add cooked chicken, wine or sherry and soy sauce; stir-fry 1 minute. Stir in cornstarch mixture; stirring constantly, cook until thickened. Serve hot. Chicken should be tender, and celery should be crisp and crunchy. Makes 4 servings.

Shredded Pork in Peking Bean Sauce

1 (1-lb. piece) boneless pork
2 cups Basic Stock, page 28
1/2 teaspoon salt
1 tablespoon crushed yellow-bean sauce
2 tablespoons rice wine or dry sherry
2 tablespoons all-purpose flour
Vegetable oil for deep-frying
1 teaspoon sugar
1 tablespoon soy sauce
1 small green bell pepper, cut into 1/2-inch pieces

1. Place pork in a medium saucepan; add stock. Bring to a boil. Reduce heat; skim off foam. Cover; simmer 25 to 30 minutes.
2. Drain pork; discard stock or reserve for another use. Cut pork into 3" x 1/2" strips. In a medium bowl, combine pork strips, salt, bean sauce, wine or sherry and flour.
3. Heat oil in a wok or deep saucepan over high heat. When oil is hot, add seasoned pork strips; deep-fry until golden. Remove pork with a slotted spoon; drain on paper towels.
4. Pour off oil. Return drained pork to same wok or skillet. Add sugar, soy sauce and green pepper; stir-fry 30 seconds. Serve hot. Makes 4 servings.

Left to right: Shredded Pork in Peking Bean Sauce, Chicken Cubes with Celery, Chicken Breast & Egg White

炸肉丸子

Shanghai Crispy Meatballs

1 lb. ground pork
1 teaspoon salt
2 tablespoons light soy sauce
1 tablespoon rice wine or dry sherry
1 teaspoon sugar
1 egg
2 teaspoons freshly ground Szechuan or black pepper
1 teaspoon finely chopped gingerroot
1 teaspoon finely chopped green onion
About 3 tablespoons cornstarch
Vegetable oil for deep-frying

1. In a medium bowl, combine pork, salt, soy sauce, wine or sherry, sugar, egg, pepper, gingerroot, onion and 2 tablespoons cornstarch. Stir 2 to 3 minutes or until blended and slightly thickened.
2. Shape pork mixture into 24 small meatballs. Coat each meatball with cornstarch.
3. Heat oil in a wok or deep-fryer over medium heat. When oil is hot, add coated meatballs, a few at a time. Deep-fry until golden. Remove meatballs with a slotted spoon.
4. Reheat oil; return cooked meatballs to oil. Deep-fry a few seconds to crisp before serving. Makes 24 small meatballs.

鴛鴦虾仁

Red & White Shrimp with Green Vegetable

2 teaspoons salt
1 lb. peeled, deveined uncooked shrimp
1 egg white
1 tablespoon cornstarch
1 cup vegetable oil
8 oz. Chinese pea pods, trimmed, or broccoli flowerets
2 green onions, finely chopped
2 teaspoons finely chopped gingerroot slices
2 tablespoons rice wine or dry sherry
1 tablespoon tomato paste
About 1 tablespoon chili sauce

This colorful dish is perfect for special occasions. As a starter, it serves 8 to 10 people. As a main dish served with 1 or 2 other dishes, it serves 4 to 6 people. Its Chinese name is Yuanyang Shrimp or Mandarin Ducks Shrimp. Mandarin ducks, also known as "love birds," are often used as symbols of affection and happiness.

1. In a medium bowl, combine a pinch of salt and shrimp. Stir in egg white; then stir in cornstarch.
2. Preheat a wok or large skillet over high heat. Add 3 tablespoons oil. When oil is hot, add pea pods or broccoli and 1 teaspoon salt. Stir-fry pea pods 1-1/2 to 2 minutes. Stir-fry broccoli 2-1/2 to 3 minutes. Place stir-fried pea pods or broccoli in center of a serving platter.
3. Wash and dry wok or skillet; place wok or skillet over high heat. Add remaining oil. When oil is hot, add coated shrimp; deep-fry 1 minute. Remove shrimp with a slotted spoon; drain on paper towels.
4. Pour off oil, leaving about 1 tablespoon in wok or pan. Add onions and gingerroot; stir-fry a few seconds. Add drained shrimp, remaining salt and wine or sherry; stir to blend. Remove half of shrimp; place at end of platter containing pea pods or broccoli.
5. Add tomato paste and chili sauce, to taste, to shrimp remaining in wok or skillet; stir a few seconds to blend sauce. Spoon shrimp mixture on other end of platter. Serve hot. Makes 4 servings.

Variation
If desired, substitute a milder Szechuan chili and tomato sauce for tomato paste and chili sauce.

糖醋大虾

Cantonese Sweet & Sour Prawns

8 oz. unpeeled prawns
1 egg white
1 tablespoon cornstarch
Vegetable oil for deep-frying
1 green onion, finely chopped
2 teaspoons finely chopped gingerroot
2 tablespoons sugar
1 tablespoon rice wine or dry sherry
1 tablespoon soy sauce
1 tablespoon vinegar
2 teaspoons cornstarch combined with
    2 tablespoons water

Like Rapid-Fried Shrimp in Shells, page 14, eat this dish with chopsticks or your fingers. Prawns are large shrimp.

1. Remove legs from prawns, but do not peel. Cut each prawn into 2 or 3 pieces. In a medium bowl, combine egg white and cornstarch. Add prawns; stir to coat.
2. Heat oil in a wok or deep saucepan over medium heat. Add coated prawn pieces, one at a time; deep-fry until golden. Remove prawns with a slotted spoon; drain on paper towels.
3. Pour off oil, leaving about 1 tablespoon in wok or pan. Add onion and gingerroot; stir-fry a few seconds. Add sugar, wine or sherry, soy sauce and vinegar. Stir constantly until sugar dissolves. Add cooked prawns; blend well. Stir in cornstarch and water mixture; stirring constantly, cook until thickened. Serve hot. Makes 4 servings.

Variation
Although it is more authentic to cook prawns unpeeled, peel before cooking, if desired.

Top to bottom: Cantonese Sweet & Sour Prawns, Red & White Shrimp with Green Vegetable

炸蟹丸子

Deep-Fried Crabmeat Balls

1 lb. fresh, frozen or canned crabmeat
2 oz. pork fat, minced
4 to 6 water chestnuts, minced
1 egg
1 tablespoon rice wine or dry sherry
1 teaspoon salt
1 tablespoon finely chopped gingerroot
1 teaspoon finely chopped green onion
2 tablespoons cornstarch
Vegetable oil for deep-frying
Lettuce leaves

1. In a medium bowl, combine crabmeat, pork fat, water chestnuts, egg, wine or sherry, salt, gingerroot, onion and cornstarch.
2. Chill mixture 1 hour to firm. Shape into 24 (1-inch) balls.
3. Heat oil in a wok or deep saucepan over medium heat. When oil is hot, add crabmeat balls, one at a time. Deep-fry until light golden. Remove crabmeat balls with a slotted spoon.
4. Increase heat to high. Return cooked crabmeat balls to oil; deep-fry a few seconds or until golden brown. Place lettuce leaves on a serving plate. Arrange hot crabmeat balls over lettuce. Makes 24 small balls.

Variations
Make and cook crabmeat balls through step 3 the day before serving. Warm as in step 4. Or, place crabmeat balls in 1/2 cup boiling stock in a wok or saucepan. Bring to a boil. Simmer 5 minutes. Thicken sauce with a mixture of 2 teaspoons cornstarch and a little water or stock. Garnish with 1 tablespoon finely chopped ham.

Substitute shrimp or a mixture of crabmeat and shrimp for crabmeat.

炸鳳尾虾

Phoenix-Tail Shrimp

8 oz. uncooked large shrimp
1/2 teaspoon salt
2 tablespoons rice wine or dry sherry
1 green onion, finely chopped
2 teaspoons finely chopped gingerroot
Vegetable oil for deep-frying
3 egg whites
1 tablespoon cornstarch
3 tablespoons all-purpose flour
1/4 cup dry breadcrumbs
1 tablespoon salt
1 tablespoon freshly ground Szechuan or black pepper
Shredded lettuce leaves

Deep-fry these shrimp with their tails still attached. The tails make the hot shrimp easy to handle.

1. Wash and peel shrimp; leave tails firmly attached. Split shrimp almost in half lengthways; devein.
2. Pat shrimp dry with paper towels. In a medium bowl, combine halved shrimp, salt, wine or sherry, onion, gingerroot and 1 teaspoon oil.
3. Heat remainder of oil in a wok or deep saucepan over medium heat. In a medium bowl, beat egg whites until frothy; fold in cornstarch.
4. When oil is hot, coat seasoned shrimp in flour. Dip floured shrimp in egg-white mixture; then roll in breadcrumbs. One at a time, lower coated shrimp into hot oil. Deep-fry in 3 or 4 batches until golden. Remove shrimp with a slotted spoon; drain on paper towels.
5. Preheat a small skillet over low heat. Add salt and pepper; heat 2 to 3 minutes. Pour into a small bowl.
6. Place lettuce on a serving plate. Arrange shrimp over lettuce. Serve with salt and pepper dip. Makes 4 servings.

三鮮海味

Three Sea Flavors — Scallops, Shrimp & Squid

4 oz. squid
4 oz. peeled, deveined uncooked large shrimp
4 sea scallops, quartered
1 teaspoon salt
1/2 teaspoon freshly ground pepper
2 teaspoons cornstarch
2 tablespoons Basic Stock, page 28, or water
1/2 cup vegetable oil
2 teaspoons finely shredded gingerroot
2 green onions, finely shredded
1 medium red bell pepper, cut into 1/2-inch pieces
3 celery stalks, cut into 1/2-inch pieces
1 carrot, halved, cut into 1/2-inch pieces
1 tablespoon rice wine or dry sherry
1 tablespoon soy sauce
1/2 to 1 tablespoon hot bean paste
1 teaspoon sesame oil

This is a colorful and delicious dish. It illustrates the harmonious contrast of Chinese cooking.

1. Prepare squid as in Stir-Fried Squid Flowers, page 50. Cut each shrimp into 2 or 3 pieces. In a medium bowl, combine prepared squid, shrimp pieces, scallops, salt and pepper.
2. In a small bowl, combine cornstarch and stock or water; set aside.
3. Preheat a wok or large skillet over high heat. Add vegetable oil. When oil is hot, add seasoned squid, shrimp and scallops; stir-fry 1 minute or until shrimp turn pink. Remove with a slotted spoon; drain on paper towels.
4. Pour off oil, leaving about 1 tablespoon in wok or skillet. Add gingerroot and onions; stir-fry a few seconds. Add bell pepper, celery and carrot; stir-fry 1 minute. Return cooked scallops, squid and shrimp to wok or skillet. Add wine or sherry, soy sauce and bean paste. Stir to blend. Stir in cornstarch mixture; stirring constantly, cook until thickened. Stir in sesame oil; serve hot. Makes 4 servings.

Clockwise from left: Fish Slices with Wine Sauce, Three Sea Flavors, Phoenix-Tail Shrimp

糟 熘 魚 片

Fish Slices with Wine Sauce

1 lb. sole fillets
1 egg white, slightly beaten
2 tablespoons cornstarch mixed with
    5 tablespoons water
Vegetable oil for deep-frying
1-1/2 teaspoons salt
1 teaspoon sugar
1 cup Basic Stock, page 28
1/4 cup rice wine or dry sherry
1 teaspoon sesame oil

Oil for deep-frying must be fresh or it will color the fish.

1. Cut fish into large pieces, leaving skin on. In a medium bowl, combine fish pieces and egg white. Stir in cornstarch mixture.
2. Heat vegetable oil in a wok or deep saucepan over medium heat. When oil is hot, add coated fish pieces, one at a time. Reserve leftover cornstarch mixture. Deep-fry coated fish 1 minute, separating with chopsticks. Remove fish with a slotted spoon; drain on paper towels.
3. Pour off oil; return cooked fish pieces to wok or pan. Add salt, sugar, stock and wine or sherry. Bring liquid to a boil. Reduce heat; simmer 2 minutes.
4. Stir in reserved cornstarch mixture. Tilt wok to distribute cornstarch mixture evenly over fish.
5. Stirring gently, cook until sauce thickens. Sprinkle with sesame oil. Serve hot. Makes 4 servings.

油爆鱿魚

Stir-Fried Squid Flowers

1 lb. squid
3 tablespoons vegetable oil
1 teaspoon finely chopped gingerroot
1 green onion, finely chopped
1 tablespoon rice wine or dry sherry
1 teaspoon salt
1 tablespoon soy sauce
1 teaspoon sugar
Green onion tops, finely sliced
Cucumber slices

---

1. Clean squid, discarding head, transparent pen and ink sac. Peel off thin outer membrane. Cut squid open. Score inside of squid in a crisscross pattern as shown below. Cut scored squid into 1-1/2" x 1" pieces. When squid is cooked, it will resemble corn-on-the-cob.
2. Preheat a wok or large skillet over high heat. Add oil. When oil is hot, add gingerroot and chopped onion; stir-fry a few seconds. Add squid pieces; stir-fry about 30 seconds. Add wine or sherry, salt, soy sauce and sugar; stir-fry 2 minutes. Do not overcook or squid will become tough.
3. Serve hot garnished with sliced onion tops and cucumber slices. Makes 4 servings.

1/Remove transparent pen and ink sac.

2/Peel off outer membrane.

3/Cut squid open.

4/Score inside in a crisscross pattern.

Top to bottom: Stir-Fried Squid Flowers, Szechuan Shrimp Chili & Tomato Sauce, Shredded Fish with Celery

干烧明虾

Szechuan Shrimp in Chili & Tomato Sauce

8 oz. peeled, deveined uncooked shrimp
1 teaspoon salt
1 egg white
2 teaspoons cornstarch
Vegetable oil for deep-frying
1 green onion, finely chopped
2 teaspoons finely chopped gingerroot
1 garlic clove, finely chopped
1 tablespoon rice wine or dry sherry
1 tablespoon tomato paste
About 1 teaspoon chili sauce
Lettuce leaves

1. In a medium bowl, combine shrimp and a pinch of salt. Stir in egg white; then stir in cornstarch.
2. Heat oil in a wok or deep saucepan over medium heat. When oil is hot, add coated shrimp, separating with chopsticks. Deep-fry 30 seconds. Remove shrimp with a slotted spoon; drain on paper towels.
3. Pour off oil, leaving about 1 tablespoon in wok or pan. Increase heat to high. Add onion, gingerroot and garlic; stir-fry a few seconds. Add drained shrimp; stir-fry a few seconds.
4. Stir in remaining salt, wine or sherry, tomato paste and chili sauce, to taste. Stir constantly until blended. Place lettuce on a serving platter. Arrange shrimp mixture over lettuce. Makes 4 servings.

酱汁鱼块

Braised Fish Steak

1 lb. cod or haddock fillets
All-purpose flour
1 cup vegetable oil
2 teaspoons finely chopped gingerroot
2 green onions, finely chopped
2 tablespoons rice wine or dry sherry
1 tablespoon sugar
1 teaspoon salt
1 tablespoon vinegar
5 tablespoons Basic Stock, page 28
1 tablespoon cornstarch mixed with a little water
1 teaspoon sesame oil

1. Cut fillets into large pieces; leave skin on fillets. Lightly dust with flour.
2. Preheat a wok or skillet over high heat. Add vegetable oil. When oil is hot, add floured fish, one piece at a time; deep-fry 1 minute. Remove fish with a slotted spoon; drain on paper towels.
3. Pour off oil, leaving about 1 tablespoon in wok or pan. Add gingerroot, onions, wine or sherry, sugar, salt, vinegar, stock and drained fish pieces.
4. Reduce heat; simmer gently 2 minutes. Stir in cornstarch mixture; stirring constantly, cook until thickened. Sprinkle with sesame oil; serve hot. Makes 4 servings.

鱼丝芹菜

Shredded Fish with Celery

8 oz. cod or haddock fillets
1 teaspoon salt
1 tablespoon rice wine or dry sherry
1 egg white
1 tablespoon cornstarch
3 or 4 celery stalks
Vegetable oil for deep-frying

To garnish:
1 oz. cooked ham, thinly shredded

1. Remove skin from fish; cut fish into thin slices. In a medium bowl, combine sliced fish and a pinch of salt. Stir in wine or sherry and egg white; then stir in cornstarch. Let fish mixture stand while preparing and cooking celery.
2. Cut celery into thin shreds.
3. Preheat a wok or skillet over high heat. Add 2 tablespoons oil. When oil is hot, add celery and remaining salt. Stir-fry about 1-1/2 minutes. Place celery in a serving dish.
4. Heat remaining oil in a wok or deep-fryer over medium heat. Deep-fry coated fish 2 minutes, separating with chopsticks. When fish floats to surface, remove with a slotted spoon; drain on paper towels. Arrange fish over celery.
5. Garnish with cooked ham. Serve hot or cold. Makes 4 servings.

魚 香 茄 子

Eggplant with Szechuan "Fish Sauce"

3 to 6 dried red chilies
1 (1-lb.) eggplant
Vegetable oil for deep-frying
3 or 4 green onions, finely chopped
1 teaspoon finely chopped gingerroot
1 garlic clove, finely chopped
1 teaspoon sugar
1 tablespoon soy sauce
1 tablespoon vinegar
1 tablespoon hot bean paste
2 teaspoons cornstarch mixed with 2 tablespoons water
1 teaspoon sesame oil

No fish is used in this recipe. The sauce normally is used for fish dishes, hence the name "fish sauce."

1. Soak chilies in water to cover 5 to 10 minutes. Drain; cut into small pieces, discarding stalks. If small, chilies can be left whole. Peel eggplant; cut into 1-1/2-inch diamond-shaped pieces.
2. Heat vegetable oil in a wok or deep saucepan over medium heat. Add eggplant pieces; deep-fry 1-1/2 to 2 minutes or until soft. Remove eggplant with a slotted spoon; drain on paper towels.
3. Pour off oil; return cooked eggplant to wok or pan. Add soaked chilies, onions, gingerroot and garlic; stir-fry a few seconds. Add sugar, soy sauce, vinegar and bean paste; stir-fry 1 minute. Stir in cornstarch mixture; stirring constantly, cook until thickened. Sprinkle with sesame oil. Serve either hot or cold. Makes 4 servings.

Variation
Add 4 ounces thinly shredded pork at beginning of step 3 before returning cooked eggplant to wok or saucepan.

Top to bottom: Stir-Fried Spinach & Bean Curd, Eggplant with Szechuan "Fish Sauce," Braised Broccoli, Stir-Fried Mixed Vegetables

菠菜炒豆腐

Stir-Fried Spinach & Bean Curd

---

8 oz. spinach
8 oz. bean curd
1/4 cup vegetable oil
1 teaspoon salt
1 teaspoon sugar
1 tablespoon soy sauce
1 teaspoon sesame oil

---

1. Wash spinach well; shake off excess water.
2. Cut bean curd into 16 pieces.
3. Heat vegetable oil in a wok or large skillet over high heat. Add bean-curd pieces; stir-fry until golden, gently turning. Remove bean curd with a slotted spoon.
4. Add spinach to wok or skillet; stir-fry 30 seconds or until leaves are limp. Add bean curd, salt, sugar and soy sauce; stir-fry 1 to 1-1/2 minutes or until blended. Sprinkle with sesame oil; serve hot. Makes 4 servings.

油燜西芝

Braised Broccoli

---

1 lb. broccoli or cauliflower
3 tablespoons vegetable oil
1 teaspoon salt
1 teaspoon sugar
3 tablespoons Basic Stock, page 28, or water

---

1. Cut broccoli or cauliflower into flowerets; peel and thinly slice stalks.
2. Preheat a wok or skillet over high heat. Add oil. When oil is hot, add broccoli or cauliflower flowerets and sliced stalks; stir-fry 30 seconds. Add salt, sugar and stock or water; cook 2 to 3 minutes, stirring constantly. Serve hot. Makes 4 servings.

炒鮮蔬

Stir-Fried Mixed Vegetables

---

4 oz. fresh bean sprouts
2 carrots
4 oz. Chinese pea pods, trimmed, or broccoli flowerets
3 tablespoons vegetable oil
4 oz. bamboo shoots, sliced
1 teaspoon salt
1 teaspoon sugar
1 tablespoon Basic Stock, page 28, or water

This dish should have harmonious contrast in color and texture.

1. Wash bean sprouts in cold water; discard bits and pieces that float to the surface.
2. Cut carrots into thin slices. If pea pods are large, cut into 2 or 3 pieces.
3. Preheat a wok or large skillet over high heat. Heat oil in preheated wok or skillet. When oil is hot, add sliced carrots, pea pods or broccoli and bamboo shoots; stir-fry 1 minute. Add washed bean sprouts, salt and sugar. Stir-fry 1 to 2 minutes, adding stock or water, if necessary. Do not overcook because vegetables will lose their crunchiness. Serve hot. Makes 4 servings.

Variations
If fresh sprouts are not available, do not used canned bean sprouts. Substitute thinly shredded celery for fresh bean sprouts.

Substitute cabbage, zucchini or cauliflower for bamboo shoots.

For stir-frying, choose the freshest vegetables available. Use as soon as possible after purchasing. To prevent loss of vitamins into water, wash vegetables before cutting. To avoid vitamin destruction by exposure to air, cook vegetables soon after cutting. Never overcook vegetables or use too much water in cooking. Do not use a lid over the wok or pan when cooking green vegetables unless specified. This will spoil the bright green color.

鍋 燒 牛 肉

Braised Beef

1-1/2 lbs. beef stew cubes, trimmed
Water
2 tablespoons rice wine or dry sherry
2 tablespoons soy sauce
1 teaspoon five-spice powder
2 thin gingerroot slices
2 medium tomatoes, halved or quartered
2/3 cup packed brown sugar
3 or 4 carrots
1 teaspoon salt

1. Place beef in a saucepan; add water to cover. Add wine or sherry, soy sauce, five-spice powder, gingerroot and tomatoes. Bring to a boil. Reduce heat; cover. Simmer 45 minutes. Add brown sugar; cook 30 minutes longer.
2. Cut carrots to same size as beef. Add carrots and salt to beef mixture. Cook 30 minutes longer or until liquid has reduced and thickened into a delicious sauce. If necessary, increase heat and remove cover.
3. Serve hot. Makes 4 to 6 servings.

Variation
Refrigerate leftovers; lift off excess fat before reheating. Flavor improves if made ahead, refrigerated and reheated.

粉 蒸 牛 肉

Steamed Beef Szechuan-Style

1-1/2 lbs. boneless beef top-round steak
1/2 cup minced green onions
2 tablespoons rice wine or dry sherry
1 to 2 tablespoons hot bean paste
1 tablespoon soy sauce
1 tablespoon minced gingerroot
1 tablespoon vegetable oil
1 teaspoon sugar
1 to 1-1/4 cups spicy rice powder
Chinese-cabbage leaves

To garnish:
Finely chopped green onion

If rice powder is not available, in a blender or food processor fitted with a steel blade, process 1 cup rice, 1 teaspoon five-spice powder and 1/2 teaspoon Szechuan or black peppercorns until finely ground.

1. Cut beef across grain into thin slices. In a medium glass bowl, combine onions, wine or sherry, hot bean paste, soy sauce, gingerroot, oil and sugar. Add sliced beef; stir. Let stand 30 minutes.
2. Meanwhile, roast rice powder in a dry skillet over low heat until aromatic and golden brown, stirring constantly. Line a steamer with cabbage leaves. Drain beef, if necessary; coat with browned rice powder. Arrange in layers over cabbage leaves.
3. Steam 25 to 30 minutes. Garnish with onion. Serve hot. Makes 4 to 6 servings.

Chill chicken or meats in the freezer 30 minutes before slicing. Chilling firms the chicken or meat. This aids in cutting the thin, even slices needed in Chinese cooking.

Left to right: Braised Beef, Steamed Beef Szechuan-Style

金华玉樹鷄

Cantonese Chicken, Ham & Greens

1 (2-1/2- to 2-3/4-lb.) broiler-fryer chicken
Water
2 thin gingerroot slices
2 green onions
2 teaspoons salt
8 oz. cooked ham
2 tablespoons vegetable oil
8 oz. broccoli flowerets or bok choy, chopped

Serve cold as a starter or as part of a buffet. Or serve it hot as a main course. When served on its own with rice or noodles, this dish is ample for 4 to 6 people.

1. Place chicken in a large saucepan; cover with cold water. Add gingerroot, onions and 1-1/2 teaspoons salt. Bring to a boil. Cover; simmer 25 to 30 minutes. Turn off heat; keep pan covered. Let steep in hot water at least 1 hour. *Do not* lift lid. Lifting lid will let heat escape, and chicken will not cook properly.
2. Heat 2 tablespoons oil in a wok or skillet. Add broccoli or bok choy and a little salt; stir-fry 2 to 3 minutes. Arrange cooked broccoli or bok choy around edge of a serving dish.
3. To serve, drain chicken. Gently pull meat from bone; cut into small pieces. Cut ham into thin slices same size as chicken pieces.
4. Arrange chicken and ham slices in alternate layers in center of serving dish. Makes 4 to 6 servings.

红 烧 鸡 块

Shanghai Braised Chicken

1 (3- to 3-1/2-lb.) broiler-fryer chicken
2 thin gingerroot slices
2 green onions
2 tablespoons vegetable oil
2 tablespoons rice wine or dry sherry
3 tablespoons soy sauce
1 tablespoon sugar
1/2 cup Basic Stock, page 28, or water
4 or 5 dried Chinese mushrooms
8 oz. bamboo shoots, sliced

Substitute 4 chicken quarters for whole chicken.

1. Cut chicken into 12 to 14 pieces. Cut gingerroot and onions into small pieces.
2. Heat oil in a wok or saucepan over high heat. Add gingerroot and onions; stir-fry a few seconds. Add chicken pieces; stir-fry 5 minutes or until chicken is lightly browned. Add wine or sherry, soy sauce, sugar and stock or water. Reduce heat; simmer 20 to 25 minutes, stirring occasionally.
3. Meanwhile, soak mushrooms in warm water 20 minutes or until softened; rinse. Squeeze dry; discard hard stems. Add mushrooms and bamboo shoots to chicken mixture. Increase heat to high; cook 10 minutes or until liquid has almost evaporated. Serve hot. Makes 4 to 6 servings.

Variation
Substitute carrots for bamboo shoots. If dried Chinese mushrooms are not available, substitute fresh mushrooms.

烩 鸡 翅

Chicken Wings Assembly

12 chicken wings, wing-tips removed
1/4 teaspoon salt
1 tablespoon sugar
2 tablespoons soy sauce
2 tablespoons rice wine or dry sherry
1 tablespoon cornstarch
2 tablespoons vegetable oil
1 garlic clove, crushed
3 green onions, cut into short lengths
3 to 4 tablespoons Basic Stock, page 28, or water
1 teaspoon sesame oil, if desired

---

1. Cut wings in half at joints as shown below. Combine wing pieces, salt, sugar, soy sauce, wine or sherry and cornstarch. Let stand 10 minutes, turning once or twice.
2. Preheat a wok or skillet over high heat. Add vegetable oil; heat. Add seasoned wings; stir-fry 1 to 2 minutes or until wings start to brown. Remove with a slotted spoon.
3. Add garlic and onions to wok or skillet to flavor oil. Add wings and a little stock or water. Stir; cover. Cook over a medium-high heat 5 minutes. Listen carefully for sizzling to make sure it is not burning. Add more stock or water, if necessary. Occasionally stir gently to prevent wings sticking to bottom of skillet or wok.
4. Cover; cook 5 to 10 minutes longer or until sauce is almost entirely absorbed. Add sesame oil, if desired, stirring to blend. Serve hot. Makes 4 to 6 servings.

1/Using a sharp knife, cut off wing-tip of each chicken wing.

2/Cut between remaining joint to make 2 pieces.

Clockwise from bottom: Chicken Wings Assembly, Shanghai Braised Chicken, Cantonese Chicken, Ham & Greens

香 酥 鴨

Aromatic & Crispy Szechuan Duck

1 (3- to 3-1/2-lb.) duck
2 teaspoons salt
4 thin gingerroot slices
3 green onions
3 tablespoons rice wine or dry sherry
1 teaspoon five-spice powder
4 star anise
2 teaspoons Szechuan or black peppercorns
Vegetable oil for deep-frying

To serve:
12 Thin Pancakes, page 76
1/4 cup Hoisin or barbecue sauce
6 green onions, cut into thin strips

This dish is claimed to be the forerunner of the world-renowned Peking Duck. It is on the menu in most Peking-style restaurants. It is eaten exactly like Peking Duck, that is, wrapped in pancakes with strips of onion and Hoisin sauce.

1. Remove and discard excess fat from duck. Split duck down back through meat and bone. Rub duck with salt. In a deep dish, combine duck, gingerroot, onions, wine or sherry, five-spice powder, star anise and peppercorns. Cover and refrigerate overnight or at least 3 hours, turning several times.
2. Place duck and marinade in deep heatproof dish. Place dish in a steamer. Steam 2-1/2 hours. Remove and discard marinated vegetables.
3. Heat oil in a wok or deep-fryer over medium heat. Add steamed duck; deep-fry 10 to 12 minutes or until brown and crispy. Remove duck; drain.
4. To serve, pull meat from bone. Spread each pancake with sauce. Top with onions and meat. Fold pancakes over filling. Makes 4 to 6 servings.

Variation
If steamer is not large enough to hold a whole duck, place duck and marinade in a large saucepan. Add 5 cups stock. Simmer 2-1/2 to 3 hours; remove from cooking liquid. Pat dry with paper towels before deep-frying.

Aromatic & Crispy Szechuan Duck with Thin Pancakes, page 76

清蒸滑鷄

Steamed Chicken with Mushrooms

1-1/2 lbs. boneless chicken breasts
1 teaspoon salt
1 teaspoon sugar
1 tablespoon rice wine or dry sherry
1 teaspoon cornstarch
3 or 4 dried Chinese mushrooms
2 thin gingerroot slices
1 teaspoon vegetable oil
Freshly ground Szechuan or black pepper
1 teaspoon sesame oil

1. Cut chicken into bite-size pieces. Combine chicken pieces, salt, sugar, wine or sherry and cornstarch. Soak mushrooms in warm water 20 minutes or until softened; rinse. Squeeze dry; discard hard stems.
2. Thinly shred mushrooms and gingerroot. Grease a heat-proof plate or dish with vegetable oil.
3. Place chicken pieces on greased plate or dish. Sprinkle with shredded mushrooms and gingerroot, pepper and sesame oil.
4. Place dish in a steamer. Steam 20 minutes or until chicken is tender. Serve hot. Makes 4 to 6 servings.

The easiest way to judge when poultry is done is to insert a meat thermometer into the inner-thigh area before roasting Roast poultry until thermometer registers 180F to 185F (80C to 85C). Or, roast until juices run clear when a knife is inserted between thigh and breast.

八宝鴨

Eight-Treasure Duck

1 cup glutinous rice
Water
1 (4- to 5-lb.) duck
3 tablespoons dark soy sauce
4 or 5 dried Chinese mushrooms
1 tablespoon dried shrimp
2 tablespoons vegetable oil
1/3 cup finely chopped green onions
1 tablespoon finely chopped gingerroot
1/2 cup cubed bamboo shoots
1/2 cup cubed cooked ham
2 tablespoons rice wine or dry sherry
Salt

To garnish:
Finely chopped green onions
Carrot slices
Parsley sprigs

Eight-Treasure refers to various ingredients used in the stuffing. If glutinous rice is unavailable, substitute short-grain rice. If desired, reserve the gizzard for stuffing.

1. Wash rice under cold running water until water runs clear. Cover with cold water; soak 6 hours or overnight. Drain rice; place in a medium saucepan. Add 2 cups water; bring to a boil. Reduce heat; cover. Cook 30 minutes or until water is absorbed. Do not remove cover during cooking. Set cooked rice aside.
2. Clean duck well inside and out; pat dry with paper towels. Brush skin with soy sauce. Set duck aside.
3. Soak dried mushrooms in warm water 20 minutes or until softened; rinse. Squeeze dry; discard hard stems. Cut mushroom caps into small cubes. Soak shrimp in warm water 20 minutes to soften. Drain shrimp; set aside.
4. Preheat a wok or skillet. Add oil. When oil is hot, add onions and gingerroot; stir-fry about 1 minute. Add mushrooms, shrimp, bamboo shoots and ham, stirring constantly. Add remaining soy sauce and wine or sherry. Stir-fry until mixture is well blended. Turn off heat; stir in cooked rice. Season with salt.
5. Preheat oven to 400F (205C). Stuff duck with rice mixture; close cavity. Place duck, breast-side up, on a rack in a pan containing several inches of water. Roast in preheated oven 30 minutes. Reduce heat to 350F (175C); roast 45 minutes longer or until duck is tender. Add more water to pan, if needed.
6. Remove stuffing from duck; cut duck into serving pieces. Arrange stuffing and duck on a large platter. Sprinkle onions over stuffing. Garnish with carrot slices and parsley. Makes 4 to 6 servings.

Left to right: Eight-Treasure Duck, Steamed Chicken with Mushrooms

酒蒸鸡

Drunken Chicken

1 (2-1/2- to 2-3/4-lb.) broiler-fryer chicken
Water
Salt
1/2 cup rice wine or dry sherry
2 tablespoons brandy
2 thin gingerroot slices
2 to 3 green onions, cut into short lengths
Freshly ground pepper

No liquid other than rice wine or dry sherry and brandy is used in cooking this dish, so it is highly aromatic. The chicken should be so tender that pieces can be easily pulled off with chopsticks.

1. Blanch chicken in a saucepan of boiling water 1 minute. Remove; rinse in cold water.
2. Place chicken, breast-side down, in a large bowl. Add 1-1/2 teaspoons salt, wine or sherry, brandy, gingerroot and onions. Place bowl in a steamer; steam 1-1/2 hours. Remove chicken; place on a serving dish, breast-side up.
3. Pour about half of cooking liquid into a saucepan; season with salt and pepper. Bring to a boil. Pour over chicken. Makes 4 to 6 servings.

清炖獅子頭

Yangchow "Lion's Head" (Pork Meatballs with Chinese Cabbage)

1-1/4 lbs. ground pork
2 teaspoons finely chopped gingerroot
2 green onions, finely chopped
1 teaspoon salt
2 tablespoons rice wine or dry sherry
1 tablespoon cornstarch
1 medium Chinese cabbage
2 tablespoons vegetable oil
1 cup Basic Stock, page 28, or beef stock

This famous dish originated from Yangchow in the Yangtse River delta. Pork meatballs are supposed to resemble the shape of a lion's head, with the cabbage its mane, hence the name.

1. In a large bowl, combine pork, gingerroot, onions, salt, wine or sherry and cornstarch. Shape mixture into 4 to 6 meatballs.
2. Cut cabbage into large chunks. Heat oil in a large saucepan. Add cabbage; stir-fry 1 minute. Place meatballs on top of cabbage; add stock. Bring to a boil. Cover; simmer 45 minutes. Serve hot. Makes 4 to 6 servings.

Variation
Add 2 tablespoons soy sauce and 1 tablespoon sugar to meatball mixture. Reduce salt to 1/2 teaspoon. Meat will have a darker, richer appearance.

五香排骨

Five-Spice Pork Spareribs

1-1/2 to 1-3/4 lbs. pork spareribs
1 teaspoon salt
1 tablespoon sugar
2 tablespoons rice wine or dry sherry
2 tablespoons soy sauce
1 teaspoon five-spice powder
1 tablespoon Hoisin or barbecue sauce

1. Cut pork into individual ribs. With a cleaver, chop each rib into 2 or 3 small pieces. In a shallow ovenproof dish, combine ribs and remaining ingredients. Cover and let stand 1 hour, turning once or twice.
2. Preheat oven to 400F (205C).
3. Bake seasoned spareribs in preheated oven 40 to 45 minutes or until tender, turning once.
4. Or barbecue ribs on a grill 15 to 20 minutes or until brown and crispy, turning once or twice. Makes 4 servings.

Variation
Substitute a mixture of 1 teaspoon chili sauce, 1 teaspoon vinegar, 2 teaspoons cornstarch and 1 crushed garlic clove for Hoisin or barbecue sauce.

豉汁蒸排骨

Cantonese Steamed Pork Spareribs in Black-Bean Sauce

1 lb. pork spareribs
1 garlic clove, finely chopped
1 teaspoon finely chopped gingerroot
1 tablespoon black-bean sauce
1 tablespoon soy sauce
1 tablespoon rice wine or dry sherry
1 teaspoon sugar
1 teaspoon cornstarch

To garnish:
2 green onions, cut into short lengths
1 small hot red pepper, thinly shredded
1 teaspoon sesame oil

1. Cut pork into individual ribs. With a cleaver, chop spareribs into small pieces.
2. In a large bowl, combine garlic, gingerroot, black-bean sauce, soy sauce, wine or sherry, sugar and cornstarch. Add chopped spareribs; let stand 15 to 20 minutes.
3. Place seasoned spareribs on a heatproof plate; put into a steamer. Steam 25 to 30 minutes or until tender.
4. Garnish with onions and red pepper. Sprinkle with sesame oil. Serve hot. Makes 2 to 3 servings.

Left to right: Yangchow "Lion's Head," Five-Spice Pork Spareribs, Cooked Rice

清蒸鱸魚

Cantonese Steamed Sea Bass

1 (1-1/4-lb.) sea bass or trout, cleaned
1 teaspoon salt
1 teaspoon sesame oil
4 green onions
3 dried Chinese mushrooms, soaked, thinly shredded
2 oz. lean pork, thinly shredded
2 tablespoons light soy sauce
1 tablespoon rice wine or dry sherry
2 teaspoons cornstarch
2 teaspoons thinly shredded gingerroot
2 tablespoons vegetable oil

1. Wipe fish with a damp paper towel. Diagonally slash both sides of fish to the bone at 3/4-inch intervals. Rub half of salt and all of sesame oil inside fish. Place 2 or 3 onions on a heatproof dish; top with fish.
2. In a small bowl, combine mushrooms, pork, remaining salt, 1 tablespoon soy sauce, wine or sherry and cornstarch. Stuff half of mixture inside fish; place remainder on top. Sprinkle with gingerroot. Place in a steamer; steam 15 minutes or until fish tests done.
3. Cut remaining onions into short lengths. Heat vegetable oil in a saucepan until hot.
4. Remove dish containing fish from steamer. Pour off about half of cooking liquid; arrange onions over fish. Top with remaining soy sauce and hot oil. Serve hot. Makes 2 to 3 servings.

糖醋全魚

Sweet & Sour Whole Fish

1 (1-1/2-lb.) sea bass or grey mullet, cleaned
1 teaspoon salt
1/2 teaspoon freshly ground white pepper
2 tablespoons rice wine or dry sherry
Vegetable oil for deep-frying
2 tablespoons cornstarch
2 tablespoons Basic Stock, page 28, or water
2 green onions, finely chopped
2 thin gingerroot slices, finely chopped
2 tablespoons sugar
2 tablespoons vinegar
1/2 teaspoon dark soy sauce
1 teaspoon sesame oil

1. Wipe fish with a damp paper towel. Diagonally slash both sides of fish to the bone at 1/2-inch intervals. Rub fish inside and out with salt and white pepper. Place seasoned fish in a shallow dish. Pour wine or sherry over fish. Let stand 30 to 60 minutes.
2. Heat vegetable oil in a wok or deep saucepan over high heat. Coat fish with about 1-1/2 tablespoons cornstarch. Deep-fry 3 minutes. Reduce heat to medium; fry another 3 minutes or until fish tests done and is golden brown. Place on a platter. In a small bowl, combine remaining cornstarch and stock or water; set aside.
3. Pour off oil, leaving about 1 tablespoon in wok or pan. Add onions, gingerroot, sugar and vinegar. Stir in cornstarch mixture and soy sauce. Cook until thickened, stirring constantly. Add sesame oil. Pour sauce over fish. Serve hot. Makes 2 to 3 servings.

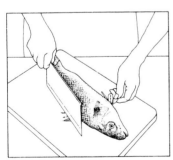
1/Cut fins from fish.

2/Remove scales by scraping from tail to head.

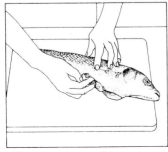
3/Remove viscera. Rinse.

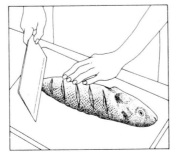
4/Diagonally cut to bone.

In China, a fish weighing less than 2 pounds is often cooked whole. The ideal size is 1-1/4 to 1-1/2 pounds. The fish is slashed on both sides to prevent skin from bursting during cooking, to allow heat to penetrate quickly and to help diffuse flavor of the seasonings. Always choose a fresh fish. The usual rules are: its eyes should be clear and full, not sunken; its gills should be bright red; the body should be firm, not flabby; and it should smell pleasantly fresh. For a perfect fish dish, do not overcook. Cooked fish should be firm and opaque, not tough and dry.

Clockwise from right: Cantonese Steamed Trout, Red Mullet in Black-Bean Sauce, Sweet & Sour Whole Fish

豉汁燒紅鯔魚

Red Mullet in Black-Bean Sauce

1 (1-lb.) red mullet or red snapper, cleaned
1 teaspoon salt
1 tablespoon cornstarch
1/4 cup vegetable oil
1 garlic clove, crushed
2 thin gingerroot slices, thinly shredded
1 small green bell pepper, sliced
2 tablespoons salted black beans, crushed
2 tablespoons rice wine or dry sherry

1. Wipe fish with a damp paper towel. Diagonally slash both sides of fish to the bone at 3/4-inch intervals. Rub inside and out with salt; coat with cornstarch.
2. Heat about half of oil in a wok or skillet. Add garlic, gingerroot and green pepper; stir-fry a few seconds. Add black beans; blend well. Remove green-pepper mixture with a slotted spoon; set aside.
3. Heat remaining oil in wok or skillet. Add fish; sauté on each side 2 to 3 minutes. Return green-pepper mixture to wok or pan. Add wine or sherry. Cook 2 to 3 minutes, carefully turning fish once.
4. Place cooked fish on a platter. Top with green-pepper mixture. Serve hot. Makes 2 servings.

干烧鱼

Szechuan Braised Fish in Chili Sauce

1 (1-1/2-lb.) sea bass, carp, grey mullet or trout
Vegetable oil for deep-frying
2 teaspoons finely chopped gingerroot
1 garlic clove, finely chopped
2 tablespoons hot bean paste
1 tablespoon soy sauce
2 tablespoons rice wine or dry sherry
1/2 teaspoon salt
3 tablespoons Basic Stock, page 28, or water
1 teaspoon sugar
2 teaspoons vinegar
2 teaspoons cornstarch mixed with 1 tablespoon water
About 1 teaspoon chili sauce

To garnish:
2 green onions, finely chopped

The amount of hot bean paste and chili sauce can either be increased or reduced according to how hot you like your food. If you have difficulty in finding hot bean paste, substitute crushed yellow-bean sauce mixed with chili sauce.

1. Wipe fish with a damp paper towel. Diagonally slash both sides of fish to the bone at 3/4-inch intervals.
2. Heat oil in a wok or deep saucepan over medium heat. Add fish; deep-fry 5 minutes, turning over once. Remove fish; set aside.
3. Pour off oil, leaving about 1 tablespoon in wok or pan. Add gingerroot, garlic, hot bean paste, soy sauce and wine or sherry; stir until blended. Return fish to wok or pan. Add salt and stock or water. Reduce heat; simmer 2 to 3 minutes. Turn fish over; add sugar, vinegar, cornstarch mixture and chili sauce, to taste. Cook until sauce is thickened, stirring constantly. Garnish with finely chopped onions. Serve hot. Makes 2 to 3 servings.

豆腐烧鱼

Fish & Bean-Curd Casserole

1 (1-lb.) cod, haddock or salmon steak
1-1/2 tablespoons all-purpose flour
3 or 4 dried Chinese mushrooms
8 oz. firm bean curd, page 69
Vegetable oil for deep-frying
1 teaspoon salt
1 teaspoon sugar
1 tablespoon soy sauce
2 tablespoons rice wine or dry sherry
2 green onions, cut into short lengths
1 tablespoon shredded gingerroot
1 cup Basic Stock, page 28

To garnish:
Fresh coriander leaves or parsley sprigs, if desired

---

1. Cut fish into 6 pieces. Coat with flour.
2. Soak mushrooms in warm water 20 minutes or until softened. Rinse; squeeze dry. Discard hard stems; cut caps in halves or quarters.
3. Cut bean curd into 8 pieces.
4. Heat oil in a wok or deep-fryer over medium heat. Add fish pieces; deep-fry 5 minutes or until fish is golden. Remove with a slotted spoon; drain on paper towels.
5. To same oil, add bean-curd pieces; deep-fry until golden. Remove with a slotted spoon; drain.
6. Place fried bean curd, fish pieces and mushrooms in a Chinese sand-pot or saucepan. Add salt, sugar, soy sauce, wine or sherry, green onions, gingerroot and stock. Bring to a boil; reduce heat. Cover; simmer 10 minutes. Garnish with fresh coriander or parsley, if desired. Serve in sand-pot or saucepan. Makes 4 to 6 servings.

The Chinese casserole known as the *sand-pot* or *sandy-pot* is made of clay. It has a coarse, sandy-textured beige exterior, often encased in a network of wire, and a dark brown, smoothly glazed interior.

Never place an empty sand-pot on the heat; there should always be liquid in the pot to prevent it from cracking. Never place a hot sand-pot on a damp or cold surface until it has cooled, or it may crack.

Left to right: Chinese-Cabbage Casserole in a sand-pot, Szechuan Braised Fish in Chili Sauce

沙鍋白菜

Chinese-Cabbage Casserole

1 large Chinese cabbage
3 or 4 dried Chinese mushrooms
1 tablespoon dried shrimp
1 lb. sliced bamboo shoots or 6 or 7 carrots, sliced
2 cups Basic Stock, page 28, or chicken stock
1 teaspoon salt
1 tablespoon rice wine or dry sherry

1. Discard tough, outer cabbage leaves; trim off hard root. Cut cabbage into 3 or 4 pieces. Place cabbage pieces in a Chinese sand-pot or saucepan.
2. Soak mushrooms and shrimp in warm water 20 minutes or until softened. Rinse mushrooms; squeeze dry. Discard hard stems. Place soaked mushrooms and shrimp on top of cabbage.
3. Place bamboo shoots or carrots on cabbage.
4. Add enough stock to half cover cabbage. Season with salt. Simmer 30 minutes over medium heat.
5. Before serving, add wine or sherry; bring to a boil. Serve hot. Makes 4 to 6 servings.

紅扒鵪鶉蛋

Braised Quail's Eggs with Mushrooms

24 quail's eggs
2 tablespoons soy sauce
2 tablespoons cornstarch
8 oz. Chinese pea pods, broccoli or asparagus
1 or 2 carrots
1 teaspoon salt
1 teaspoon sugar
1 teaspoon sesame oil
1 cup Basic Stock, page 28, or chicken stock
Vegetable oil for deep-frying
1 (15-oz.) can straw mushrooms, drained, or 8 oz. fresh
  mushrooms

1. Put eggs in a medium heatproof bowl; add cold water to cover. Place bowl in a steamer; steam 10 minutes. Remove eggs; plunge into cold water 5 minutes. Shell cooked eggs. In a medium bowl, combine eggs and soy sauce. Let stand 20 minutes, turning frequently. Remove eggs; reserve soy sauce. Coat eggs with 1 tablespoon cornstarch.
2. Trim and string pea pods or cut broccoli or asparagus and carrots into 2- to 3-inch lengths.
3. In a small bowl, combine salt, sugar, sesame oil, remaining cornstarch, stock and reserved soy sauce; set aside.
4. Heat vegetable oil in a wok or deep saucepan over medium heat. When oil is hot, add eggs; deep-fry until golden. Remove with a slotted spoon; drain on paper towels.
5. Pour off oil, leaving about 2 tablespoons in wok or saucepan. Add trimmed pea pods, cut broccoli or asparagus and carrots with about 1/3 of sauce mixture. Stir-fry 1-1/2 to 2 minutes. Arrange cooked vegetables around edge of a serving dish.
6. Add 2 tablespoons oil to wok or saucepan. Heat until hot. Add mushrooms; stir-fry 30 seconds. Add deep-fried eggs and remaining sauce; stir gently. When sauce thickens, pour egg mixture into center of vegetables. Serve hot. Makes 4 to 6 servings.

Variation
Substitute 1 (15-ounce) can quail's eggs for fresh eggs. Can contains about 30 quail's eggs already cooked and shelled. Drain off water; omit steaming and shelling.

Top to bottom: Cantonese Crab Cooked in Black-Bean Sauce, Bean Curd with Assorted Meats, Braised Quail's Eggs with Mushrooms

什錦豆腐

Bean Curd with Assorted Meats

8 oz. firm bean curd, cut into 20 cubes
2 oz. cooked ham, diced
4 oz. fresh mushrooms, diced
4 oz. bamboo shoots, diced
4 oz. cooked pork, beef or lamb, cut in small cubes
1 cup Basic Stock, page 28, or beef stock
1/2 teaspoon salt
1 tablespoon soy sauce
8 oz. broccoli flowerets or coarsely chopped bok choy
2 tablespoons vegetable oil
4 oz. peeled, deveined cooked small shrimp

Any leftover roasted meat is perfect for this dish.

1. In a medium saucepan, combine bean curd, ham, mushrooms, bamboo shoots and meat. Add stock, salt and soy sauce. Slowly bring to a boil. Cook uncovered over low heat 1 hour.
2. Just before serving, heat oil in a wok or large skillet. Stir-fry broccoli or bok choy in hot oil 1-1/2 to 2 minutes. Arrange stir-fried broccoli or bok choy around edge of a serving dish.
3. Spoon bean-curd mixture into center of serving dish; top with shrimp. Makes 4 to 6 servings.

豉椒焗螃蟹

Cantonese Crab Cooked in Black-Bean Sauce

2 (1- to 1-1/4-lb.) cooked crabs
1 tablespoon soy sauce
2 tablespoons rice wine or dry sherry
1 tablespoon cornstarch
3 tablespoons vegetable oil
1 garlic clove, finely chopped
4 thin gingerroot slices, finely chopped
2 to 3 green onions, finely chopped
2 tablespoons fermented black-bean sauce, crushed
1 tablespoon vinegar
2 to 3 tablespoons Basic Stock, page 28, or water

This dish is best eaten with your fingers. Provide a bowl of warm water with a slice or two of lemon in it as a finger bowl.

1. Break each crab into 3 or 4 pieces, separating legs and claws. Crack shells. Discard feathery gills and bile sac.
2. In a large bowl, combine soy sauce, wine or sherry and cornstarch. Add crab pieces; let stand 10 minutes.
3. Preheat a wok or skillet. Add oil; heat. Add garlic, gingerroot and onions; stir-fry 1 minute to flavor oil. Add black-bean sauce, stirring until smooth. Add seasoned crab; stir-fry 1-1/2 to 2 minutes. Add vinegar and stock or water. Continue stirring until thickened. Serve hot. Makes 4 servings.

Fresh bean curd, sealed in a small container and packaged under the name *tofu*, is extremely soft and silky. It does not absorb other flavors as readily as the firmer types that are available from Oriental specialty stores. Tofu tends to fall apart in stir-frying. Therefore, it is not suitable for most Chinese cooking, except for soup recipes. If only soft bean curd is available, blanch it 2 to 3 minutes to harden the texture, so that it will be firm enough to stir-fry. Freezing bean curd will toughen it and give it a honeycomb-like texture. Or slice fresh bean curd and place between clean kitchen towels. Top with a flat object and weights for 30 to 60 minutes. This will press out moisture and firm bean curd. It is then more suitable for slow, long-cooking methods.

1/Remove legs and claws.

2/Crack claws by striking with back of cleaver.

3/Crack shell into 2 to 3 pieces.

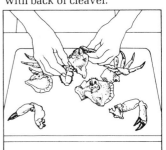

4/Discard feathery gills and bile sac.

什錦火鍋

Chinese Hot-Pot

1 lb. lean lamb, pork, beef or combination
8 oz. boneless chicken breasts, skinned
8 oz. peeled, deveined uncooked shrimp or fish fillets
    or 4 oz. each
8 oz. fresh mushrooms
1 lb. Chinese cabbage or spinach
8 oz. bean curd
8 oz. transparent (cellophane) noodles or
    1 lb. egg noodles
6 cups Basic Stock, page 28, or water

Dip Sauce:
6 tablespoons soy sauce
2 teaspoons sugar
1 teaspoon sesame oil
3 or 4 green onions, finely chopped
3 thin gingerroot slices, finely chopped

A Chinese hot-pot is like a fondue pot. Actual cooking is done at the dining table by each individual. Also known as Mongolian fire-pot, a Chinese hot-pot has a funnel at the center in which charcoal is burned. The moat is filled with boiling stock or water. Each individual cooks meat and vegetables in the boiling liquid, then dips it in sauce before eating.

1. Slice meat and chicken as thinly as possible; arrange separately on a large plate or together in small individual dishes.
2. Cut shrimp or fish into small slices. Thinly slice mushrooms; cut cabbage or spinach and bean curd into small pieces.
3. Soak transparent noodles until soft, if using. Arrange all ingredients on a platter or in separate dishes.
4. Combine ingredients for Dip Sauce; pour into 6 to 8 small bowls. Each person should have a bowl of sauce.
5. Bring stock or water to a rapid boil. Using chopsticks or a fondue fork, let each person pick up a piece of meat of his or her choice and dip it into the boiling liquid 1 to 2 minutes. When meat changes color, it is done. Remove from boiling liquid, dip into sauce and eat while piping hot.
6. When all meats have been eaten, add all vegetables and noodles to hot liquid. Boil a few minutes; ladle into individual bowls. Season soup with remaining Dip Sauce. This makes a delicious soup to finish the meal. Makes 6 to 8 servings.

Chinese Hot-Pot

Rice, Noodles & Pancakes

什錦炒面

Fried Noodles with Assorted Meats (Chow Mein)

4 oz. peeled, deveined uncooked shrimp
4 oz. fresh bean sprouts
2 or 3 eggs
Salt
1/4 cup vegetable oil
1 lb. Chinese egg noodles
Water
2 to 3 green onions, cut into 2-inch lengths
4 oz. lean pork, shredded
4 oz. cooked ham, shredded
2 carrots, shredded
4 oz. Chinese pea pods or green beans, trimmed
1 teaspoon sugar
1 tablespoon rice wine or dry sherry
2-1/2 tablespoons soy sauce

1. If using large shrimp, cut into 2 or 3 pieces. Leave smaller shrimp whole.
2. Wash bean sprouts; set aside.
3. In a small bowl, beat eggs with a pinch of salt. Preheat a wok or large skillet over medium heat. Add 1 tablespoon oil. When oil is hot, pour in beaten eggs; spread to make a large, thin egg pancake. Carefully turn to cook other side. Place on a cutting board; cool slightly. Cut egg pancake into thin strips.
4. Cook noodles according to package directions. Drain; rinse with cold water. Set aside.
5. Heat remaining oil in wok or skillet over high heat. Add onions, pork, ham, shrimp, carrots, washed bean sprouts, pea pods or beans, sugar and wine or sherry. Stir-fry over high heat 1 minute. Add noodles, egg strips and soy sauce. Continue stirring until all ingredients are distributed. Serve hot or cold. Makes 6 to 8 main-dish servings or 10 to 12 cold-buffet servings.

汤面

Noodles in Soup

8 oz. boneless chicken, pork or lamb, shredded
Salt
2 teaspoons cornstarch
12 oz. Chinese egg noodles
2 cups Basic Stock, page 28, or chicken stock
3 tablespoons vegetable oil
2 or 3 green onions, cut into 2-inch lengths
2 teaspoons shredded gingerroot
4 oz. fresh mushrooms, shredded
4 oz. bamboo shoots, shredded
1/2 cucumber, sliced
3 tablespoons light soy sauce
1 tablespoon rice wine or dry sherry
2 teaspoons sesame oil, if desired

1. In a medium bowl, combine chicken or lamb, 1/2 teaspoon salt and cornstarch; set aside.
2. Cook noodles according to package directions. Drain; do not rinse in cold water.
3. Place noodles in a large serving bowl or 4 individual bowls.
4. In a medium saucepan, bring stock to a boil; pour over cooked noodles.
5. Preheat a wok or skillet. Add vegetable oil. When oil is hot, add onions and gingerroot; stir-fry a few seconds. Add chicken or meat, mushrooms, bamboo shoots and cucumber. Stir a few times; add 2 tablespoons soy sauce, wine or sherry and salt to taste. Cook 1 to 1-1/2 minutes, stirring constantly. Pour mixture over noodles. Season with remaining soy sauce and sesame oil, if desired. Serve hot. Makes 4 servings.

Top to bottom: Fried Noodles with Assorted Meats (Chow Mein), Noodles in Soup

什錦 燴飯 (廣東式)

Cantonese Rice

8 oz. squid
4 oz. bay scallops
1 lamb or veal kidney
2 teaspoons cornstarch
1/4 cup water
4 oz. green beans, trimmed
Boiling water
1/4 cup coarsely chopped green onion
1/2 cup shredded cooked pork roast
3 tablespoons vegetable oil
2 tablespoons soy sauce
1 teaspoon sugar
Salt
2 teaspoons sesame oil, if desired
4 cups hot cooked long-grain white rice

This is a popular Cantonese dish known as Mixed Meats or Assorted Meats with Rice. Ingredients vary according to the cook's whims or available ingredients. This recipe is only a suggestion; add or substitute, if desired.

1. Prepare squid as for Stir-Fried Squid Flowers, page 50.
2. Rinse scallops; drain.
3. Prepare kidney as for Stir-Fried Kidney Flowers Shandong-Style, page 43.
4. In a small bowl, blend cornstarch and water until smooth; set aside.
5. In a large saucepan, blanch prepared squid and kidney pieces, rinsed scallops and beans in boiling water 10 to 15 seconds. Drain; set aside.
6. Preheat a wok or large skillet over high heat. Add vegetable oil. When oil is hot, add squid, scallops, kidney, beans, onions and pork; stir-fry 1 minute. Add soy sauce, sugar and salt to taste; stir a few times. Stir in cornstarch mixture. Cook 2 to 3 minutes or until thickened, stirring constantly. Add sesame oil, if desired. Serve hot over cooked rice. Makes 4 to 6 servings.

什錦炒飯

Yangchow Fried Rice

3 or 4 dried Chinese mushrooms or
    2 oz. fresh mushrooms
4 oz. peeled, deveined uncooked shrimp
2 or 3 eggs
1 teaspoon salt
2 green onions, finely chopped
3 tablespoons vegetable oil
1/2 cup finely diced bamboo shoots or
    1/2 cup finely diced carrots
1/2 cup uncooked green peas or
    1 small green bell pepper, finely diced
1/2 cup finely diced cooked ham or pork
2 to 3 cups cold cooked white rice
1-1/2 tablespoons light soy sauce

This popular dish may have originated in the river port of Yangchow on the Yangtse delta. It is on the menu of almost every Cantonese restaurant. The ingredients can be substituted or varied, if desired. If possible, use cooked rice that is cold and hard. If rice must be cooked for this dish, let cool before using.

1. If using dried mushrooms, soak in warm water 20 minutes or until softened; rinse. Squeeze dry; discard hard stems. Dice into small cubes. If using fresh mushrooms, leave small ones whole; dice large ones. If shrimp are large, cut into 2 or 3 pieces. Leave small shrimp whole.
2. Lightly beat eggs. Beat in a pinch of salt and half the onions.
3. Preheat wok or skillet over medium heat; add 1 tablespoon oil. When oil is hot, add eggs; scramble. Remove scrambled eggs with a spatula; set aside.
4. Heat remaining oil in same wok or skillet over high heat. Add all vegetables, shrimp and ham or pork; stir-fry 1 to 2 minutes. Add cooked rice, salt and soy sauce. Stir to separate each grain of rice. Add scrambled eggs, breaking into small pieces. Serve hot. Makes 4 servings.

炒米粉

Fried Rice Noodles

1 lb. rice noodles
1 tablespoon dried shrimp
1/4 cup vegetable oil
1/2 cup shredded bamboo shoots
4 oz. lean pork, shredded
2 celery stalks, sliced
4 green onions, shredded
1 teaspoon salt
1/4 cup Basic Stock, page 28, or water
2 tablespoons light soy sauce

It has not been established who first made noodles, the Chinese or Italians. However, noodles have been eaten in China for more than 2000 years.

Also known as rice sticks, rice noodles are very popular in southern China. They can be substituted in most recipes for noodles made from wheat flour.

1. Soak rice noodles in warm water 10 to 15 minutes or until soft. Soak dried shrimp in warm water 20 minutes or until softened.
2. Preheat a wok or skillet over high heat. Add 2 tablespoons oil. When oil is hot, add soaked shrimp, bamboo shoots, pork, celery and onions; stir-fry 1 to 2 minutes. Add salt and stock or water; cook about 2 minutes. Spoon pork mixture into a medium bowl. Wash and dry wok or skillet.
3. Add remaining oil to wok or skillet. Drain rice noodles; add to wok or skillet. Stir to coat each noodle with oil. Add soy sauce and pork mixture. Stir constantly 1-1/2 to 2 minutes or until no liquid is left.

Variation
Singapore Fried Rice Noodles: Substitute 1 small white onion, chopped, for celery; add 2 teaspoons curry powder with soy sauce. If desired, substitute narrow dried egg noodles, spaghetti or spaghettini for rice noodles.

Top to bottom: Fried Rice Noodles, Yangchow Fried Rice, Cantonese Rice

Thin Pancakes

2 cups all-purpose flour
3/4 cup boiling water
Sesame oil

These pancakes are traditionally served with dishes such as Aromatic & Crispy Duck, page 58, or Mu-Shu Pork, page 41. Serve them with any dish of your choice. Pancakes can be made well in advance. Before serving, steam 5 minutes to reheat. Use refrigerated leftovers within 3 or 4 days or freeze up to 6 months.

1. Sift flour into a large bowl. Gradually add boiling water, blending with a wooden spoon.
2. Knead dough on a lightly floured surface until firm and smooth. Cover kneaded dough with a damp cloth; let rest 20 minutes. Shape dough into a 12-inch rope. Cut rope into 12 (1-inch) pieces. Using heel of hand, flatten each piece into a 2- to 3-inch circle. Brush 1 side of each circle with a little sesame oil. Place oiled sides together, making 6 sandwiches.
3. Using a rolling pin, roll each sandwich on a lightly floured surface to a 6-inch pancake, rolling gently on both sides. Do not roll edges too thin or pancakes will not separate after cooking.
4. Place an ungreased skillet over medium heat. Place 1 pancake at a time into skillet. When pancake starts to puff up with air bubbles, turn over. Cook until little brown spots appear on underside. Gently peel layers apart. Fold each pancake in half; keep warm under a damp cloth until ready to serve. Makes 12 pancakes.

Peking Onion Pancakes

3 cups all-purpose flour
1 cup boiling water
Sesame oil
Salt
1 cup thinly sliced green onions
1/4 cup vegetable oil

---

1. Sift flour into a large bowl. Gradually add water, blending with a wooden spoon. Knead dough on a lightly floured surface until firm and smooth. Cover kneaded dough with a damp cloth; let rest 20 minutes.
2. Shape dough into a 12-inch rope. Cut into 12 (1-inch) pieces. With a rolling pin, roll each piece on a lightly floured surface into a flat pancake about 7 inches in diameter. Brush generously with sesame oil. Sprinkle salt and 1 tablespoon onion over each pancake. Tightly roll each pancake; seal ends. Shape each rolled pancake into a spiral; gently press flat with palm of your hand. Let flattened spirals stand a few minutes. Roll spirals into 6-inch circles on a lightly floured surface.
3. Heat vegetable oil in a skillet over medium heat; add pancakes, one at a time. Fry 5 to 6 minutes or until golden brown and crisp, turning once. Serve with soup or other dish. Makes 12 pancakes.

Variation
Substitute 1 large or 2 medium coarsely chopped onions for green onions.

1/Brush one side of each pancake with a little oil. Stack two pancakes, oiled sides together to form a sandwich.

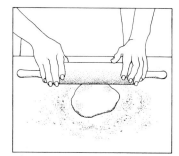

2/Using a rolling pin, roll out each sandwich on a lightly floured surface. Roll gently on both sides to form a 6-inch circle.

春 捲 (上海式)

Shanghai Spring Rolls

20 egg-roll skins
2 teaspoons cornstarch
1 tablespoon soy sauce
1 tablespoon rice wine or dry sherry
8 oz. lean pork, finely shredded
5 or 6 dried Chinese mushrooms
3 tablespoons vegetable oil
1 cup shredded bamboo shoots
1-1/2 cups finely chopped green onions
Salt
1 teaspoon sugar
1 egg white
Vegetable oil for deep-frying

Dip Sauce:
2 tablespoons rice vinegar
2 teaspoons thinly shredded gingerroot

Shanghai Spring Rolls do not contain bean sprouts. They are ideal for a buffet or cocktail snacks.

1. Remove egg-roll skins from package; defrost, if necessary. Cover with a damp cloth to prevent drying.
2. In a medium bowl, combine cornstarch, soy sauce and wine or sherry until smooth. Add pork; stir to combine. Let stand 20 to 30 minutes.
3. Soak dried mushrooms in warm water 20 minutes or until softened. Rinse; squeeze dry. Discard hard stems; thinly shred caps.
4. Preheat a wok or skillet over medium heat. Add 3 tablespoons oil. When oil is hot, add seasoned pork; stir-fry until lightly browned. Remove pork with a slotted spoon; set aside. Add shredded mushrooms, bamboo shoots and onions to same wok or skillet. Stir-fry about 1 minute. Add salt, sugar and cooked pork. Stir-fry 1 minute. Cool pork mixture before using.
5. To make spring rolls, spoon 1 to 2 tablespoons filling on bottom corner of 1 egg-roll skin. Fold lower corner of skin over filling; roll once. Brush side corners with egg white; fold both sides in toward center. Roll again. Brush upper corner of skin with egg white. Roll into a tight package. Repeat with remaining skins and filling. Place spring rolls on waxed paper; cover with a towel until ready to deep-fry. These can be refrigerated 1 day or frozen up to 3 months.
6. Heat oil in a wok or deep-fryer. Add spring rolls a few at a time. Deep-fry 3 to 4 minutes or until golden and crisp. Remove deep-fried rolls with a slotted spoon; drain on paper towels. Prepare Dip Sauce by combining vinegar and gingerroot in a small bowl. Serve sauce with hot spring rolls. Makes 20 rolls.

Left to right: Peking Onion Pancakes, Thin Pancakes, Shanghai Spring Rolls

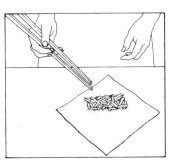
1/Place filling on egg-roll skin.

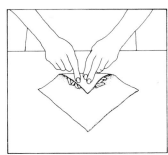
2/Place lower corner over filling.

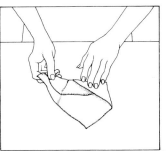
3/Fold in both sides; roll again.

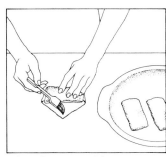
4/Brush corner with egg white before final rolling.

豆沙包

Steamed Dumplings with Savory Fillings

1 recipe Dumplings, opposite recipe

Filling:
1/2 lb. boneless pork, diced
1 cup coarsely chopped bamboo shoots
1/2 cup coarsely chopped green onions
2 tablespoons soy sauce
2 tablespoons rice wine or dry sherry
2 tablespoons Basic Stock, page 28, or water
2 teaspoons sugar
1 teaspoon sesame oil
1 teaspoon finely chopped gingerroot
Salt
4 to 6 Chinese-cabbage leaves

Dip Sauce:
2 tablespoons soy sauce mixed with
   1 tablespoon vinegar

1. Prepare dumpling dough as in previous recipe, rolling into 3-inch circles.
2. To make filling, in a medium bowl, combine pork, bamboo shoots, onions, soy sauce, wine or sherry, stock or water, sugar, sesame oil, gingerroot and salt.
3. Place about 1-1/2 tablespoons filling in center of each dough circle. Gather dough over filling, pinching and pleating on top. Twist top tightly to enclose filling. Place 1 inch apart on waxed paper. Cover with a damp towel. Let rise in a warm place, free from drafts, 30 minutes or until doubled in bulk.
4. Line a steamer rack with cabbage leaves. Place dumplings 1 inch apart on leaves. Cover; steam 20 minutes or until dough is cooked. Serve with Dip Sauce. To reheat leftovers, steam 5 minutes or shallow-fry, page 9, in a little oil 5 to 6 minutes. Makes 14 dumplings.

小笼肉包

Steamed Dumplings with Sweet Filling

Dumplings:
1 (1/4-oz.) package active dry yeast (1 tablespoon)
2 teaspoons sugar
3/4 cup warm water (110F, 45C)
2-1/2 to 3 cups all-purpose flour

Filling:
1 cup canned sweet red-bean paste

1. In a large bowl, dissolve yeast and sugar in warm water. Let stand until foamy, 5 to 10 minutes. Stir in 2 to 2-1/2 cups flour or enough to make a soft dough. Turn out dough on a lightly floured surface. Knead in enough remaining flour to make a stiff dough. Knead dough 5 to 8 minutes or until smooth and elastic.
2. Shape dough into a 14-inch rope. Cut dough into 14 (1-inch) pieces. Flatten pieces with heel of hand. With a rolling pin, roll out each piece on a lightly floured surface into a 3-inch circle.
3. Place 1 tablespoon bean paste in center of each circle. Gather dough over filling, pinching and pleating on top. Twist top tightly to enclose filling. Place 1 inch apart on waxed paper; cover with a damp cloth. Let rise in a warm place, free from drafts, 30 minutes or until doubled in bulk.
4. Transfer waxed paper and dumplings to a steamer rack. Cover and steam 15 to 20 minutes or until dough is cooked. Serve hot. Makes 14 dumplings.

Variation
Top each dumpling with 1/2 teaspoon bean paste before steaming.

1/Roll dough into a rope.

2/Cut; flatten each piece.

3/Place filling in center of dough.

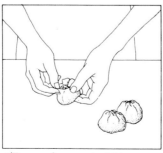
4/Draw edges up; twist to enclose.

白 飯

Plain Boiled Rice

2 cups long-grain white rice
4 to 5 cups water

1. Rinse rice in cold water.
2. Place rinsed rice and 4 cups water in a medium saucepan. Bring to a boil over medium heat. Stir occasionally to prevent rice sticking to bottom of pan.
3. Reduce heat to very low. Cover; cook 15 minutes or until rice is tender. Add more water, if necessary. Turn off heat; let rice stand 10 minutes. All water should be absorbed.
4. Before serving, fluff rice with a fork or spoon. Makes 6 cups cooked rice.

Variation
Substitute other types of rice, if desired. Cook according to package directions.

Clockwise from top: Steamed Dumplings with Sweet Filling, Plain Boiled Rice, Steamed Dumplings with Savory Filling

Index